A GALAXY OF THINGS

A Galaxy of Things explores the ways in which all puppets, masks, make-up-prosthetic figures are "material characters," using iconic Star Wars characters like Yoda and R2-D2 to illustrate what makes them so compelling.

As an epic franchise, Star Wars has been defined by creatures, droids, and masked figures since the original 1977 movie. Author Colette Searls, a theatre director and expert in puppetry studies, uncovers how non-humans like Chewbacca, semi-humans like Darth Maul, and even concealed humans like Boba Fett tell meaningful stories that conventional human characters cannot. Searls defines three powers that puppets, masked figures, and other material characters wield—distance, distillation, and duality—and analyzes Star Wars' most iconic robots and aliens to demonstrate how they work across nearly a half-century of live-action films. Yoda and "Baby Yoda"—two of popular culture's greatest puppets—use these qualities to transform their human companions. Similarly, Darth Vader's mask functions as a performing object driving mystery and suspense across three film trilogies. The power of material characters has also been wielded in problematic ways, such as stereotypes in the representation of service droids and controversial creatures like Jar Jar Binks. Bringing readers forward into the first Star Wars live-action streaming series, the book also explores how the early 2020s stories centered material characters in particularly meaningful, often redemptive ways.

A Galaxy of Things is an accessible guide to puppets, masks, and other material characters for students and scholars of theatre, film, puppetry, and popular culture studies. It also offers useful perspectives on non-human representation for researchers in object-oriented ontology, posthumanism, ethnic studies, and material culture.

Colette Searls is an Associate Professor of Theatre at the University of Maryland, Baltimore County (UMBC), USA, where she teaches acting, directing, and puppetry. She is an award-winning puppetry artist and has received grants from the Jim Henson Foundation and Puppeteers of America for her original works in object theatre.

A GALAXY OF THINGS

The Power of Puppets and Masks in Star Wars and Beyond

Colette Searls

Routledge
Taylor & Francis Group

LONDON AND NEW YORK

Designed cover image: © Photo by www.mitchelwutoyphotography.com

First published 2023
by Routledge
4 Park Square, Milton Park, Abingdon, Oxon OX14 4RN

and by Routledge
605 Third Avenue, New York, NY 10158

Routledge is an imprint of the Taylor & Francis Group, an informa business

© 2023 Colette Searls

British Library Cataloguing-in-Publication Data
A catalogue record for this book is available from the British Library

Library of Congress Cataloging-in-Publication Data
Names: Searls, Colette, author.
Title: A galaxy of things : the power of puppets and masks in Star Wars and
beyond / Colette Searls.
Description: Abindon, Oxon ; New York : Routledge, 2023. | Includes
bibliographical references and index.
Identifiers: LCCN 2022060862 (print) | LCCN 2022060863 (ebook) | ISBN
9780367684433 (hardback) | ISBN 9780367684419 (paperback) | ISBN
9781003137559 (ebook)
Subjects: LCSH: Star Wars films--Miscellanea. | Characters and
characteristics in motion pictures. | Costume. | Masks in motion
pictures. | Film makeup.
Classification: LCC PN1995.9.S695 S255 2023 (print) | LCC PN1995.9.S695
(ebook) | DDC 791.43/75--dc23/eng/20230327
LC record available at https://lccn.loc.gov/2022060862
LC ebook record available at https://lccn.loc.gov/2022060863

ISBN: 9780367684433 (hbk)
ISBN: 9780367684419 (pbk)
ISBN: 9781003137559 (ebk)

DOI: 10.4324/9781003137559

Typeset in Bembo Std
by KnowledgeWorks Global Ltd.

This book is dedicated to my many Searls parents,
talented writers all:

Esther Searls (Mom)

Doc Searls (Pop)

Janet Searls (Aunt Gigi)

Joyce Searls (Situ)

CONTENTS

ACKNOWLEDGMENTS

The resources of time, funds, space, personnel support, research materials, and infrastructure for this book came from the University of Maryland, Baltimore County (UMBC). UMBC sits on the unceded land of the Susquehannock and Piscataway peoples. To all past, present, and future Indigenous people connected to this place, I offer my humble respect.

This project was supported by the UMBC College of Arts, Humanities, and Social Sciences (CAHSS) via a CAHSS Research Fellowship, and a Center for Innovation, Research, and Creativity in the Arts (CIRCA) Research Fellowship. I am grateful to Prof. Lynn Cazabon, director of CIRCA, and to the CAHSS leaders who worked to increase such essential support for faculty research, particularly in the arts: Dean Kimberly Moffit and Dean Emeritus Scott Casper. I'd like to acknowledge my colleagues at the UMBC Department of Theatre, especially our Business Services Specialist, Ms. Laurie Newton, and our Department Chair, Prof. Eve Muson. I thank my longtime colleague, Prof. Emeritus Lynn Watson, for taking over my department chair duties so that I could take a sabbatical and begin this research.

Thanks to Prof. Jodi Kelber-Kaye and Prof. Julie Oakes for inviting me to be a UMBC Honors College Faculty Fellow, enabling me to teach courses on the evolving topic of this book. The undergraduate students in both seminars helped shape my thinking through our lively discussions—I am grateful to them all.

I could not have completed this project without two dedicated research assistants. Claudia Talbot's editing, analytical conversations, and eagerness to share her encyclopedic knowledge of Star Wars were all simply invaluable. Jennie Hardman worked closely with me in the final stages of this book to bring just the right article to me at the right time, gather together my references, proof-read, and support me in every way to the finish line. UMBC students Anthony Alessandrini, Patricia "Patch" Hatley, Duncan McAdam, Emily O'Keefe, and Daniyar Sheets also provided valuable research assistance.

I'd like to thank those who coached, advised, and otherwise supported the writing process, especially Laura Holliday and T. Berkeley Goodloe at the Academic Writer's Studio, who saw me through this project from the earliest conception to the final moments of manuscript preparation. Thanks to the staff at Routledge Press and Alamy for their assistance and availability to me and my many questions. I owe a great debt to draft reviewers: Steve Abrams, Chris Ernest Hall, Amanda Petefish-Scrag, Gina Mitchell, Claudia Orenstein, Christian Pirnot, Robert Polawski, Paulette Richards, and Doc Searls. Thank you for the time you took to offer such thoughtful and formative feedback; it made a tremendous difference.

To my lifelong friend, Jennifer Scheper Hughes: thank you for your encouragement to get started on this book, your moral support to continue, and your unflinching editorial hand to finish it.

A heartfelt thanks goes to the puppetry community, especially all of the volunteers for UNIMA-USA and Puppeteers of America. Thank you for all the work you do to organize puppetry festivals, symposia, panels and—above all—for being such a fun bunch of folks. I can't wait to see you again.

Thanks most of all goes to my spouse, Todd Carpenter. Thank you for calming me with your perennially loving ear and the balm of your professional expertise. To our kids, Simon and Amalie: I have loved our family Star Wars nights, and I have relied on many of your smart ideas for this book. Thank you for understanding how important this project has been to your mom. I love you.

PREFACE

There's something irresistible about a pair of argumentative robots, a mysterious masked man with buttons for a chest, and a little green creature who talks backwards and lifts spaceships with his mind. My attraction to characters like R2-D2, Darth Vader, and Yoda has expanded outward to the whole notion of Star Wars creation, the roots of which are beautifully documented through their original concept art in large, colorful books like Phil Szostak's *The Art of Star Wars: The Force Awakens*. This and other books in *The Art of Star Wars* series teem with the strange and wondrous; my favorites include a giant bejeweled worm, a droid with an old slide projector for a head, and a gang of people who appear to be made of cloth and breathing tubes. These images project an imaginative whimsy, grounded in thoughtful amalgamations of old and new ideas inspired by real and fantastical sources. Paging through these books in recent years has reminded me of browsing an aquarium full of colorful undersea creatures, or a zoo. In these drawings, I sensed a kind of love for creating varied forms of sentient, intelligent life, as well as different versions of human beings. Clearly, these beautiful, made-up Star Wars creatures have something special to offer, something beyond the reach of human characters working alone. As a puppetry artist and scholar, I realized that analyzing Star Wars figures could offer an accessible way to explain what non-human and semi-human characters are so good at, what makes them so moving and essential.

People often said to me, as I was writing this book, that they did not realize there were puppets in Star Wars. The truth is that I consider a much broader swath of figures—masks, suits, costumes, and face-altering combinations of prosthetics and makeup—although in the beginning I did not have a collective name for them. In the Introduction to this book, I propose the term *material character* to encompass this type of performing figure—the non-human, semi-human, and concealed human. This book outlines the particular powers they wield, using Star Wars material characters as case studies and objects of analysis. The way Star Wars material characters have used their powers to contribute to this pop culture artifact has been a rich and revealing exercise. R2-D2, Yoda, and Darth Vader are examples of some of the finest achievements in creature effects and design in cinematic history, but this is not a book about special effects. It is about how Star Wars creatures, droids, and masks reveal material characters as *meaning-makers*.

I have biases, or perhaps perspectives, in putting Star Wars and material characters together. My relationship to both Star Wars and to puppetry has a lot to do with my age. Star Wars was part of a larger pop culture phenomenon saturated by made-up creatures in the 1970s, when I was growing up. I was born the week *Sesame Street* premiered, a few months after puppeteer Mr. (Fred) Rogers testified before congress to save children's public television funding. *Sesame Street*—like *Mister Rogers' Neighborhood*—was broadcast on public television, so any kid in the USA with access to a television (whose local station included the programming) could sing about their feelings with Daniel Striped Tiger, learn to count with The Count, and sound out letters with Cookie Monster. *The Muppets Show* and *Star Wars* would arrive together in the mid-1970s, and their non-human stars would begin their takeover of popular culture with more movies and television appearances, magazine covers, interviews, and toys. For myself and my friends, these characters were our play, and (better still), our parents loved them too. We of Generation X were *raised by puppets*.

I still love Star Wars as an adult, but it's different. As I write these words, I am halfway through the most recent Star Wars streaming series—which my family and I watch together on designated "Star Wars night." The thrill I feel in watching these shows isn't an echo of my experience as a kid watching the original Star Wars trilogy in the theaters, nor nostalgia for that experience (fun as it was), but the way it always puts me on the edge of surprise. I sit there awaiting some strange new droid or oddly shaped creature about to step around the corner, or pop out of the ground. I never know what's coming, but it's nearly always delightful. What *is* that, and what's it going to do? Is that droid broken? Is it happy? Can I have one?

In this book, I try to keep hold of that delight as I analyze the material characters of Star Wars, and use them as a case study. Contemporary puppet theatre scholarship is the theoretical foundation for this study because most puppetry analysis to date focuses on live performance. Of course, recorded media like film is very different from live performance, but puppet theatre scholarship is rich and expansive enough to work remarkably well. I rely heavily on the work of three puppet theatre scholars, who together edited the excellent anthology *The Routledge Companion to Puppetry and Material Performance*:

Dr. John Bell, Dr. Claudia Orenstein, and Dr. Dassia Posner. Their introductions to this volume, as well as their wider contributions to the field, have provided some of the most formative theory for my research here. I am also reliant on Penny Francis's *Puppetry: A Reader in Theatre Practice,* Dr. Eileen Blumenthal's *Puppetry: A World History,* and the recent research of Dr. Paulette Richards, which has helped me see ways the term material character can be useful beyond performance.

I also draw on my own experiences working with puppets and theatrical masks; my background as an acting instructor, stage director, and deviser of puppet performances undergirds my perspective and sense of how "things" perform. For two decades I've taught acting, puppetry, and directing as a professor of theatre at the University of Maryland, Baltimore County (UMBC), where I have led seminars on the works of Jim Henson and the analysis of material characters in Star Wars. In my own creative practice, I devise original live performances with a mixture of designed puppets and things I find, often falling into the genre of "junk puppetry," which involves animating things like plastic bags, egg cartons, and packaging material. I love to puppeteer the dull, used-up, and ignored—and this may be part of what has drawn me to write about Star Wars. Characters in this galaxy are also scavengers who invent things out of repurposed objects and other people's trash—an aspect of what I call in Chapter 1 the *Star Wars thing aesthetic.*

It's important to note that my sources on Star Wars are deliberately varied—I rely on a range of books, essays, select reviews, articles, documentaries, online entertainment features, video essays, fan websites, official websites, encyclopedias, and blogs. I make some reference to general responses from fandom, though I have not conducted studies or surveys of my own. I have cited sources for any interpretation of Star Wars that did not spring out of my own analytical work or perspective, but given the ubiquity of Star Wars as a topic of popular culture discussed in countless media platforms around the globe, and ease of posting any views anytime, it is impractical for me to catch where an idea of my own might overlap with what someone else has come to and publicly shared, and it's likely many do.

Part of the point I'm making about material characters—that they are not just about one performer, but a multitude of collaborators—makes it difficult to appropriately credit their design, construction, and performance. Most material characters in Star Wars cannot be attributed to a single creator or performer. They generally began in concept art, springing from conversations between directors and writers, undergoing numerous iterations and revisions, selections and eliminations. Historically, a team of sculptors, special effects experts, designers and technicians have weighed in throughout the process of Star Wars creature and droid creation. A practical material character in Star Wars is often performed before the camera by one or more actors, stunt experts, puppeteers, or operators, then further enhanced or built upon by voice actors and effects artists before audiences behold them on screen. C–3PO might be minimally credited to four individuals: he was conceived in concept art by Ralph McQuarrie, sculpted and designed by Liz Moore and Brian Muir, and performed by Anthony Daniels—and his case is one of the simplest. To attempt to credit, thoroughly and accurately, the wide array of talented concept artists, sculptors, model builders, writers, puppeteers, and operators collectively responsible for these characters, has proven not only impractical, but potentially unfair or even erroneous. So in this book I generally name the performer most closely (or initially) aligned with each character the first time it is mentioned, and encourage readers to peruse not only IMDb for further credits, but also my bibliography for books, articles, and documentary series that explain the significant contributions of artists and craftspeople like Christian Alzmann, Doug Chiang, Stuart Freeborn, Hal Hickel, Abbigail Keller, Phil Tippett, Liz Moore, Ralph McQuarrie, Tony McVey, Neal Scanlan, Terryl Whitlatch and many, many others.

This book uses Star Wars to illuminate in clear and simple terms the power material characters hold—in live and recorded media. I also hope the analyses here will inspire respect for objects, and further analysis of our relationship to them. Star Wars is a delightful way in to analyzing our reactions to performing *things* that are attractive to us, but decidedly not us—because their strangeness does not just make compelling stories; it makes meaning.

FIGURE 0.1 C-3PO on Tatooine in the first Star Wars film (LUCASFILM)

INTRODUCTION

The first lines uttered in *Star Wars* were spoken not by a human character but rather by a beautiful, animate thing. Though he has no flesh, his eyes are soulful. "Did you hear that? They shut down the main reactor. We will be destroyed for sure" (Lucas 1977). This photograph captures C-3PO's appearance in the original film after he escaped onto the hot surface of Tatooine, and suddenly found himself out of his element. His metal skin is covered in grime, leaking oil from bolts shaped like tender nipples. C-3PO (Anthony Daniels) is only one of countless suits, puppets, masks, and weapons-with-faces that populate the massive pop culture artifact called Star Wars. Together with his companion R2-D2 (Kenny Baker) and the other Star Wars stuff—ancient spaceships, strange tools, and magical lightsabers—these characters deliver to us a familiar-yet-exotic galaxy "far, far away."

Creatures and droids are central to Star Wars; the most famous ones, such as Yoda and Darth Vader, are recognizable throughout the globe and enduringly influential. Yet—like so many other pop-culture puppets and puppet-adjacent figures—these types of characters tend not to receive serious credit for their artistic potential and contributions to the work. In his 2015 book, *Star Wars FAQ*, Mark Clark compares some of the films' non-human performances to those of the actors nominated for Oscars in 1981, the year *Episode V: The Empire Strikes Back* (1980) was eligible for consideration: "All of these were fine performances, but none one of them have left the kind of impact on popular culture as Yoda, Darth Vader, or C-3PO" (Clark 2015, 347). There is also little attention paid to how similar they are to one another as a *type* of character. This is perhaps due to the human-centered Hollywood viewpoint, which echoes what we see in theatre in the West. As theatre historian John Bell writes in his book *American Puppet Modernism*, "In mainstream

DOI: 10.4324/9781003137559-1

Euro-American academic thinking, puppetry is somewhere on the low end of a hierarchy of theatrical forms that generally places realistic actors' theatre on the top" (Bell 2013, 14–15). Yet there are things a material character can do that the human actor performing without material cannot. Whether they appear in live theatre or film, material characters are often—and certainly in Star Wars—much more than charming sidekicks and plot devices, however much they excel in these vital functions. The purpose of this book is to name those special abilities and reveal how they both create meaningful stories and resonate beyond them. I accomplish this by using Star Wars as a case study to identify simple terms for these powers. Readers should walk away able to recognize, explain, and apply these terms and ideas to their own endeavors as creative artists, scholars, teachers, or fans of performing arts, media, and popular culture.

Our Non-Human Guides to the Galaxy of Things

Material characters in Star Wars are our hosts. With them, we will travel from a place without robots and light-speed spaceships, to one in which both are perfectly ordinary. Spencer Kornhaber, pop culture writer for *The Atlantic*, notes that "George Lucas has long said that he envisioned Star Wars as a story told from the perspective of a robot" (Kornhaber 2018). The irony is that of this droid duo, the more person-like character (C-3PO) proves the less mature and thoughtful one; his rather hapless personality creates an intriguing balance between him and the capable appliance that R2 appears to be.

Material characters like the droids also time-travel with us. Unlike science fiction that imagines the future, Star Wars is about the past—the *long ago* past—so there is an immediate sense of the historical. And yet it's filled with human-kind's dreamed-about technological inventions for the future. Kornhaber calls its universe "one of the most fertile speculative civilizations ever dreamed up, appearing at once ancient but futuristic, lived-in but supernatural, and vast but intricate" (Kornhaber 2018). Audiences can cross into that fantasy world and experience it as someone else's distant past, where they'll have no responsibility or control. To make it sweeter, the phrase "a long time ago ..." also feels like the beginning of a "once upon a time" bedtime story, or fairy tale, which may feature fantastical creatures. It's the monsters, talking animals, and robots—realized as puppets and other types of material characters—who host us on this Star Wars journey, because they are built for travel. As theatre scholar Kenneth Gross writes, puppetry "crosses between worlds and ferries us between worlds" (Gross 2014, xxiii).

C-3PO and R2 met *Star Wars'* first audience in theatres in 1977, inviting humans to both relate to and wonder at them. Their marginal status as not-alive beings was part of their power to compel our attention. C-3PO is just strange enough to create a kind of bridge: he certainly sounds like a person, and his body and face share human shape, but all visual signals confirm he's a metal robot. With very human-like responses to the catastrophe befalling him, C-3PO presents a halfway point between the "us" of humans and the very non-human bleeping dome beside him. He translates R2's language for the audience by responding to him in English, which is both humorous and meaningful. Translating us into this world is, in a way, his character's directive, as he makes clear in his formal introduction to Luke Skywalker (Mark Hamill) in the first film: "I am C-3PO. Human-cyborg relations." He is here to embody strangeness and convey us through it.

Creatures and droids also help ground Star Wars as an epic. Star Wars has been thoroughly analyzed as a myth, but I find it more useful to connect it to this larger theatrical tradition of global storytelling, one which often relies on the engagement of non-humans in performances. Star Wars is certainly an epic; the original Star Wars trilogy (1977–1983)—which actually was part of a large, complex story in Lucas's mind—has since led to a seemingly endless stream of comic books and novels as well as films and streaming series. The magazine *Puppetry International* devoted its fall 2021 issue to epic storytelling, and the journal's historian, John Bell, points to Star Wars characters in his article "Unbounded in Time: Puppets and Epics." Bell lists examples of puppetry's centuries-old presence in epic performances around the world, from Indonesia to Guatemala, but also draws readers' attention to its presence in Western popular culture: "*Star Wars, The Lord of the Rings,* the Marvel Universe, endless arrays of Netflix and Amazon Prime mini-series, *Sesame Street* … all based on the long-form repetitions and changes of epic structure" (Bell 2021, 4). Bell offers three reasons why puppetry and epics pair well. His first, "the reassurance of repetition," is particularly interesting to consider with Star Wars in mind:

> We like to see familiar characters represent consistent traits in slightly different contexts: Elmo is always friendly, Chewbacca is faithful … and Sun Wukong, the Monkey King, is always causing trouble. We don't know exactly what these characters will do in any one episode, but their consistency is something we can count on.
>
> *(Bell 2021, 6)*

This gets right to the heart of the epic Star Wars-watching experience. C-3PO has been in ten live-action Star Wars films, covering three generations of the Skywalker family story. That repetition, that reliable visit from the same friend, is part of the comfort and delight that sends audiences back to Star Wars (often with our own kids, or with our inner child), building a chain of shared, intergenerational attachment to these stories. Bell's second reason is the "vastness of their scope …. Epics amount to a whole and different world which we can temporarily visit again and again," one which is "rich and full" and often expresses the community's deepest values while offering entertainment. Puppets by their nature lead us directly into a world of strangeness, which supports Bell's third reason for the puppetry–epics relationship: "puppetry's innate desire and ability to give us that world." Bell suggests that puppetry "always wants to burst forth in creation of complex worlds that are *like ours* in some ways, but thankfully, *not* ours in our essence. And thus puppetry is always striving for something 'unbounded in time'" (Bell 2021, 6). What could be more Star Wars than this?

Material Characters Defined

The mask, the puppet, and their kindred—indeed, all figures in live-action who perform the non-human, semi-human, or concealed human—are in essence *material characters*. I offer the term as a way to collectively consider not only puppets, masks, and other performing objects, but also actors wearing face-altering prosthetics or creature suites, and animations that appear in live-action films. All of these are encompassed within my framework. This inclusive scope allows us to regard these forms as a collective, as well as discrete types. I define the material character as any figure brought to imagined life through a performer's collaboration with a thing or image. Here I draw a distinction between two broad types of characters. In the unadorned human-character group, actors with exposed faces perform fictional people who look like them, sometimes with cosmetic enhancement. In the material character group, we see every other sentient (or sentient-behaving) figure: the non-human, semi-human, and concealed human. In the first category, a person performs another person, using their own body and voice as their primary material. Figures in the latter group require at least one performer collaborating with material, or images, to create the character's identity.

Of course, all types of performances routinely involve a human actor working with tangible *stuff* such as makeup, props, costumes, and accessories. But once a performer begins to collaborate with things or images in such a way as to change, conceal, or even generate visual identity, particularly if material covers or transforms their face, we enter a new territory. Whether perennially or momentarily, that actor is performing a material character. Consider two Star Wars characters on either side of this binary as an example. Actor Samuel L. Jackson performs Jedi Master Mace Windu in *Star Wars Episode I: The Phantom Menace* (1999) wearing robes and perhaps a touch of makeup. Rosario Dawson plays former Jedi Ahsoka Tano in the live-action series *The Mandalorian* (2019–) with prosthetics and makeup that alter her face and body. Mace Windu is unadorned beyond his costume; he's recognizable as a person. In contrast, Ahsoka's striped skin and head appendages (called *lekku*) make her rather unlike a familiar human. Dawson's face and head are transformed by the makeup and prosthetics to achieve a character with some of the same powers as masked and puppeteered figures who are likewise a step or two away from an unaltered person. Ahsoka Tano is therefore a material character, by my definition.

The Puppet and the Mask

In considering this broad swath of figures—masks, suits, costumes, and face-altering combinations of prosthetics and makeup—I ground the term material character in what my own field of theatre offers as types of performance that require extending beyond the actor's flesh: the puppet and the mask. Because I support my analysis with puppetry scholarship and analyze the use of masks in this book, I will take some time to define both.

There are many types of puppets—listed in the Bibliography are books that illuminate the varieties—and many scholars have wrestled with a single definition of "puppetry." Part of the struggle is how differently this art form is regarded across the world. In the modern mainstream United States, the culture in which Star Wars emerged, puppetry has generally been considered children's fare. In much of the rest of the world, puppets and masks participate in revered performing arts traditions and ancient cultural practices; some of the oldest and most elaborate puppet performances can be found in Asian, African, and indigenous American cultures. Japanese bunraku puppetry, which dates back centuries, remains one of the most elaborate and sophisticated performing art forms in the world today. There are hundreds of international puppetry festivals hosted in countries throughout the world every year. The past several decades have seen a surge of interest in puppetry studies as many theater scholars, as well as scholars from other fields such as literature and semiotics, have analyzed the powers and qualities of the puppet and puppet-adjacent figure, often in the context of Western prejudice against it as a serious art form. There has been robust discussion and writing about what a puppet is – its function, purpose, scope, and meaning. The editors of the 2014 collection of writings on puppetry, *The Routledge Companion to Puppetry and Material Performance*, define puppetry as "the human infusion of independent life into lifeless, but not agentless, objects in performance" (Posner 2014, 5). Of the various definitions offered by scholars, I find this one most useful because it opens the door quite broadly to what a puppet might be, while turning attention to what it *does,* which is the interest of this study.

Masks are a particularly potent type of material character because they present a face, and because they have so many functions. The mask can wander the streets or tread the stage, enacting its power to transform the wearer and fool onlookers for artistic, ritualistic, or even functional purposes (like robbing a bank). My perspective on the mask as a performing thing is inspired by puppetry scholars like Penny Francis and Stephen Kaplin. Francis calls the mask a cousin to the puppet (Francis 2012, 35), and Kaplin's model for the field of study, "A Puppet Tree" (Kaplin 1999, 31), situates the mask along a continuum of puppetry: between the actor playing a character, and body (suit) puppet. *The Longman Anthology of Drama and Theatre: A Global Perspective* (which, surprisingly, features a photograph of Darth Vader's face in its section on masks) lists five functions of the mask that I find helpful to ground my analysis of their powers as material characters. To paraphrase, they are to transform the individual into something or someone else (often with mysterious or even spiritual effect), to liberate the wearer's identity through concealment (thereby emboldening their actions), to encourage audience imagination in accepting what's not real, to act as a metaphor in establishing a character as symbol, and to exist as an aesthetic object even when not performed (Schultz, Pomo, and Greenwald 2001, 14–15).

By gathering together the mask, the puppet, and other performing objects under the collective term *material character*, I aim to demonstrate their shared power. The term material character is practical to use, but also disruptive. It challenges the hierarchy between the realistically performed human and non-human that has prevailed in popular film, and American mainstream theater, by unifying these types and cultivating deeper attention to them. The term is meant to be a fluid, inclusive, and expansive tool for analysis that builds on contemporary puppetry scholarship. In the Introduction to *The Routledge Companion to Puppetry and Material Performance*, Dassia Posner writes that the collection "forays into new territory, into 'material performance': performance that assumes that inanimate matter contains agency not simply to mimic or mirror, but also to shape and create" (Posner 2014, 5). By offering the use of the noun "material character" I build upon Posner's assertion that the performing figure holds power as a thing. All material used for performance—and here I mean material that is not flesh—can hold dramatic potency both different from, and independent of, the performers who bring it to life. I join Posner and other contemporary puppetry scholars in considering how material works *with* a performer, not *for* them, and can sometimes even project meaning independently of, or beyond them. In the course of this book, I aim to make clear that material characters "shape and create" a great deal in films like Star Wars precisely because of their status as pretend beings made of images and tangible *stuff*.

Star Wars' material characters should be recognized for their contributions. Instead of looking at R2-D2 as merely a successful practical effect, and Darth Vader as simply a great costume character well-performed, I ask that we see them as kindred, and hold together in our minds all of the creatures, masked people, and dynamic objects that make Star Wars, in order to better understand and credit what meaning they generate. In doing this, I hope to inspire deeper consideration and easier analysis of all types of material characters wherever they appear.

Star Wars Scope

This book focuses on the most widely recognized elements of live-action Star Wars: the eleven Star Wars feature films (three trilogies and two standalone films) and the first of the live-action streaming series on Disney+, *The Mandalorian* (2019–) and its companion series, *The Book of Boba Fett* (2021–22). While basic knowledge of Star Wars is assumed here, readers don't need to watch or review these films to understand the examples in this book—but if you choose to see a live-action Star Wars film or streaming series for the first time in reading this, know that there are spoilers throughout. A live-action film can include animated characters (and in Star Wars often does), but the style is based on actors and real objects recorded in performance. I do not consider in this study any of the fully-animated shows, such as *The Clone Wars* and *Rebels* TV series, even though their stories often intersect meaningfully with live-action plots, themes, and characters. In these animations, everything is rendered in a unifying style, whereas live-action mingles the real with the pretend—the person and the object or CGI character—so that is where I confine this analysis.

Throughout the chapters, I reference the films first by both their episode number and title (for example, *Episode V: The Empire Strikes Back*), and thereafter I'll sometimes use a common, shorter version of the title. For ease of reference, there is a Star Wars Live-Action Guide in the appendix listing the films' release dates and names of the lead creatives. I encourage readers unfamiliar with a referenced character or scene to call up images and videos online—the ease of doing so is one of the reasons Star Wars is such a helpful case study. For example, where Chapter 4 analyzes how masks enable the Snoke/Kylo Ren confrontation in *Episode VIII: The Last Jedi*, readers can easily reference images from the film, or call up the 4-minute clip online, or via a streaming service. Bear in mind that most pre-2012 Star Wars films differ in places from what original moviegoers saw with respect to creature effects. Lucasfilm has repeatedly revised and re-released their prior works, often incorporating additional creatures or swapping characters out for different versions. These changes have no significant impact on this study; the insertions of purely animated characters into films made prior to that existing technology are fairly obvious, and curious readers can find lists of these changes with a very quick online search.

To readers who have watched or read the many Star Wars stories beyond live-action: please know that I'm aware that characters like Chewbacca and Darth Vader—indeed, nearly all Star Wars characters large and small—have complex, extended fictional lives and backstories beyond what we see in live-action. I respect this broader world of the Star Wars universe, and I'm certain that in reading the analyses of these characters there will be times when revelations and stories from the novelizations and (certainly) the animated series will bring to mind ideas that may support or counter a particular point or argument about one or more characters. Because I'm interested in how material characters operate as they manifest in performance, I only consider what characters do and say in live-action Star Wars—they are the scope of this book.

Naming the Things

The Star Wars world hasn't always been consistent about what to call the creatures and droids which are manifested via various live-action effect techniques, such as animatronics and costumes. Chewbacca (Peter Mayhew) is, for example, variously referred to as a "costume" and a "suit." The stormtroopers wear "helmets" but these function also as masks. This slippage reveals that the potency of these materials is not easily contained within a singular or obvious use or purpose. This would suggest that perhaps we do not yet quite understand what, in fact, they are. Neither do they fit well into the traditional divides of human actor-oriented performance. The categories I offer provide clarity that derives from the material character perspective. My analysis sometimes aligns with terms frequently deployed by the film industry, such as "practicals" and "performance capture." Helmet-masks are actual things; soldiers around the globe have worn a range of helmets that cover the face in part or whole for centuries, and many of the Star Wars designs drew inspiration from real historical artifacts and armor. But, to my knowledge, I am the first to refer to and consider the Star Wars stormtroopers as "helmet-mask characters." That is to say that this book draws on vocabulary that is common to the Star Wars world, even as it introduces new terms. Below, I suggest simple definitions of key terms used in this book in order to parse and make accessible the Star Wars performing things. Divided into two broad categories, practical characters are those rendered by tangible material, while digital characters are created by computer-generated imagery (CGI) animation.

Practicals

Makeup-prosthetic characters such as live-action versions of Ahsoka (Rosario Dawson) and Darth Maul (Ray Park) work with material applied directly to the skin of the actor to change or extend the human body.

Puppets in Star Wars, such as Yoda and Jabba the Hutt as they appear in *Episode VI: Return of the Jedi*, are operated by one or more puppeteers who are either concealed within, behind, or under the puppet (as in theater), and/or operated in part or whole via a remote operator/puppeteer using animatronics. These are sometimes enhanced or supported by CGI effects.

Stop motion is a type of practical puppetry achieved by the mechanism of film to create the illusion of movement. This is often regarded as a type of practical animation. Creatures like the Tauntauns in *Episode V: The Empire Strikes Back* (1980) are at times stop-motion, when shown at a distance, and other times puppets when shown close up. Stop motion use gave way to smoother effects in later films but has since been revisited for authentic tangibility and perhaps nostalgia, as in the return of the Millennium Falcon "Dejarik" chess-game-like creatures in *Episode VII: The Force Awakens* (2015).

Suit characters conceal the actor's head and other body parts, usually the whole body, to create the illusion of a bipedal being. Examples include Chewbacca and humanoid droids in the original trilogy. These are similar to makeup and prosthetic characters in the way they are anatomically aligned with their performers limb-for-limb: arm is arm, leg is leg. This results in a non-human or semi-human creature or machine.

Helmet-mask characters are created by actors playing humans or humanoids whose identities are linked to a particular mask that conceals their head and face (Darth Vader, Boba Fett, the stormtroopers). The helmet-mask has the dual purpose within the Star Wars fiction to protect and conceal (and to protect through concealment), and it's both separable from the character and essential to their identity. A character like Kylo Ren (Adam Driver) may at times don a mask and walk about as a material character just for those moments they are wearing it. So it can be permanent or fluid, but the presentation of that character is altered by the helmet-mask both for the audience and within the fiction. It is meaningful that their face (which communicates thoughts, emotions, identity, and human-ness) is both obscured and replaced by a fixed, artificial face.

Finally, there is what I call the **super-vibrant object,** non-sentient things that are life-like but not living in this fictional universe—they may appear alive, but for the most part don't act on their own—they are under the control of others. The enormous Imperial Walkers, the plucky Millennium Falcon spaceship, and the relic-like burned mask of the late Darth Vader are some of Star Wars' many super-vibrant objects. While these types of performing objects are not attached to or interacting with a human performer in the same way as those described above, and are therefore not really material characters per se, they are also not just props. They invite us to consider the synergy of organic and inorganic life. The tension of this ironic distinction is part of their charm.

Digitals (CGI)

Many characters are created from CGI. These are animated images that are meant to appear as real, such as the Gungans and the multitude of robotic battle droids in the Star Wars prequel films. They employ a range of tools, including motion capture technology (sensors in a suit that the actor wears to "capture" their movement and record it for the animation). "Mocap" technology has advanced substantially in recent decades to include detailed facial tracking. Actor Andy Serkis specializes in these "performance capture" characters who use this mocap technology, often to animate intelligent animals or humanoid creatures, and sometimes enable the actor to see the corresponding animated image they are, essentially, puppeteering in real-time. In Serkis's performance of Snoke in *Episode VIII: The Last Jedi*, for example, the voice and movement are driven by the actor, so that he collaborates directly with the image. The face of the character is intermixed with that of the actor in a way that is sometimes referred to as "digital makeup." I like to think of a performance capture character as a suit character of the imagination. CGI is also often used to enhance the capacities of a practical character by overlaying or replacing a part of their practical body with animation. Phoebe Waller-Bridge performed the droid L3-37 in *Solo* (2018) on set wearing a suit that combined pieces of the robot (on her head and body) with green fabric and an exposed face. This setup allowed the effects artists to render a character driven by the actor's physical and vocal choices with other live actors on set.

In naming these Star Wars material character types, I hope to identify the capacities held by a range of material characters and to make it easier to reference and understand them, rather than to suggest strict delineations. R2-D2 appears to be one character, but he's actually several different things/images: sometimes he's a puppet operated by remote control and/or inhabited by puppeteer (Kenny Baker) from the inside, and sometimes he's a CGI animation. This is a common approach. Some Star Wars characters are created by a combination of tools or approaches that makes them difficult to categorize; this ambiguity is part of the fun. In the original trilogies, Darth Vader is both suit *and* a helmet-mask character, and yet when he removes the mask to reveal Anakin Skywalker, he is neither.

Chapter Guide

Chapter 1 moves through all live-action Star Wars feature films and the first two streaming series from 1977 to 2022, in release order, to demonstrate how material characters have shaped this epic. I introduce what I call the *Star Wars thing aesthetic*, established in the 1970s, and analyze how it has impacted the material characters as they have evolved over the past 45+ years. Chapter 2 describes the three powers material characters can wield—distance, distillation, and duality—analyzing selected Star Wars characters in live-action scenes to demonstrate how they work. Chapters 3 and 4 deep-dive into examples of the most successful puppets and masks in Star Wars, using Yoda and Vader as central subjects, then offering comparisons to analyze what these characters inspired, respectively, in the puppet Baby Yoda (Grogu) and Kylo Ren's mask. Chapter 5 unpacks how material characters have represented harmful notions of the "Other" in Star Wars and how more recent diversifying of the fictional galaxy has coincided with centering material characters in potentially redemptive ways.

References

Bell, John. 2013. *American Puppet Modernism: Essays on the Material World in Performance*. New York, NY: Palgrave Macmillan.

Bell, John. 2021. "Unbounded in Time: Puppets and Epics." *Puppetry International*, Fall and Winter, (50): 4–6.

Clark, Mark. 2015. *Star Wars FAQ: Everything Left to Know About the Trilogy That Changed the Movies*. Milwaukee, WI: Hal Leonard.

Francis, Penny. 2012. *Puppetry: A Reader in Theatre Practice*. New York, NY: Bloomsbury Academic.

Gross, Kenneth. 2014. "Foreword." In *The Routledge Companion to Puppetry and Material Performance*, edited by Dassia N. Posner, John Bell, and Claudia Orenstein, xxiii. New York, NY: Routledge.

Kaplin, Stephen. 1999. "A Puppet Tree: A Model for the Field of Puppet Theatre." *TDR*, 43 (3) (Autumn): 28–36.

Kornhaber, Spencer. 2018. "'Solo' Droid L3-37 Is the First Woke Bot of 'Star Wars.'" *The Atlantic*, May 27, 2018. https://www.theatlantic.com/entertainment/archive/2018/05/the-soul-of-solo-is-a-droid/560969/.

Lucas, George, director. 1977. *Star Wars: Episode IV—A New Hope*. Screenplay by George Lucas. Lucasfilm Ltd.

Posner, Dassia N. 2014. "Introduction; Material Performance(s)." In *The Routledge Companion to Puppetry and Material Performance*, edited by Dassia N. Posner, John Bell, and Claudia Orenstein. New York, NY: Routledge.

Schultz, Roger, Roberto Darío Pomo, and Michael L. Greenwald. 2001. *The Longman Anthology of Drama and Theater: A Global Perspective*. Edited by Michael L. Greenwald. London, UK: Longman.

1

THE THINGS IN THE GALAXY

What Creatures, Droids, and Masks Mean to Star Wars

In the original trilogy, Lucasfilm established a way of working with objects and creatures that would ultimately grow into interconnected stories upon stories. This chapter begins by describing a collection of approaches to the live-action films and TV series, what I call the *Star Wars thing aesthetic*—the context within which material characters operate in this fictional galaxy. The second section explores all of the live-action Star Wars to date (1977–2022), unpacking how each film added to minute yet important choices within the journey from practical effects (original trilogies) to CGI (prequels), to a combination of the two (sequels and TV series).

First, it may help to offer some backstory context to the live-action Star Wars timeline. In the mid-1970s, George Lucas created *Star Wars*, whose unexpected success supported the completion of a full trilogy. The first film was later renamed *Star Wars Episode IV: A New Hope*, followed by *Episode V: The Empire Strikes Back* (1980), and *Episode VI: Return of the Jedi* (1983). Years later, another trilogy, nicknamed "the prequels," would showcase evolving methods of CGI, which George Lucas's special effects company, Industrial Light and Magic (ILM) also used to remaster the original films. So the 1990s saw a resurrection of Star Wars mass enthusiasm, particularly with the much-anticipated first prequel film *Episode I: The Phantom Menace* (1999). The first new Star Wars film to play in theaters since 1983, *Phantom Menace* was aimed at a young audience, and for many kids, it was their introduction to Star Wars. Lucasfilm focused its Star Wars output after the prequels on animation, such as *The Clone Wars* series. After Disney purchased Lucasfilm in 2012, a new generation of Star Wars creators (a term I use to refer to the collective body of producers, writers, directors, designers, artists, and effects supervisors) planned to reintroduce live-action Star Wars films to the theaters.

DOI: 10.4324/9781003137559-2

These creators included veterans of the two trilogies and/or animated series, such as executive producer Kathleen Kennedy and art director Doug Chiang. *Star Wars Episode VII: The Force Awakens* (2015), *Episode VIII: The Last Jedi* (2017), and *Episode IX: The Rise of Skywalker* (2019) constitute the "sequel trilogy," rounding out what's often called the Skywalker Saga: the story of Anakin, Luke, Leia, and their offspring. Disney released two other standalone films (*Rogue One: A Star Wars Story* in 2016 and *Solo: A Star Wars Story* in 2018) between the main sequel movies so that for five years the public could go see a new Star Wars film in the theaters once a year. These films brought Star Wars back into popularity and launched what appears, at this date, to be a perennial epic series, primarily because of the success of the Disney+ streaming service launched in November 2019 with the first live-action Star Wars series, *The Mandalorian*. Its story is set shortly after the events of the original trilogy, spread out over eight episodes that share the overall look and feel of a Star Wars feature film. *The Mandalorian* was popular and critically successful, so more seasons, and several more streaming series, have since been produced. The second streaming series, *The Book of Boba Fett* (2021–2022) includes characters from *The Mandalorian* and intersecting stories, which I examine more closely in Chapter 5. At this writing, there have been four live-action streaming series released, and there are many more in the pipeline.

The Star Wars Thing Aesthetic

Today's Star Wars creators are perennially tasked to identify that special *something* that makes Star Wars so compelling, so very *Star Wars-esque*, as they design, write, and begin to build its next live-action project. Lucas himself seemed to have lost his sense of his own magic for creating a galaxy of interactive creatures and droids in making the prequels, given the response by many critics and fans who found the CGI off-putting. Years later, the trilogy sequel creators clearly referred back to the original trilogy aesthetics, rather than those of the more recent prequel, to try to recapture some of its qualities. Filmmaker and critic Lev Grossman visited the *Episode VII: The Force Awakens* shoot, interviewed members of the cast and creative team, and titled his resulting 2015 *TIME* magazine cover article: "A New Hope: How J.J. Abrams Brought Back Star Wars Using Puppets, Greebles and Yak Hair." Grossman describes how this team of Star Wars creators were reviving Star Wars' original dirty, scruffy, aged, wires-showing look—what Lucas called the feel of a "used universe" (Grossman 2015, 73). After watching some early footage, Grossman reported that the new Star Wars "has the dustiness and feel of ancient history. It catches you up in a double-reverse …. Abrams is engaged in a kind of cinematic archeology, digging back in time, in search of that original, primal dream" (Grossman 2015, 63). Star Wars' material characters proved to be walking embodiments of this effort, not only in that first reboot, *Episode VII: The Force Awakens*, but in those to come. These Star Wars creators seem to understand how much live-action needs its material characters, particularly the practical ones, to create a sense of place in Star Wars. The way creatures, droids, and masked figures help make the Star Wars galaxy meaningful and consistent across a range of different writers, designers, and directors is especially clear when viewed from a distance at the 45+ years of Star Wars live-action creation.

Like the larger swath of design choices they belong to (set, costumes, props, vehicles, etc.) material characters thrive in Star Wars' particular world: a galaxy where things and people have binding affection and interdependent relationships. Will Brooker, author of the B.F.I. Film Classics book, *Star Wars*, points to George Lucas's own relationship to cars as a young mechanic, noting that "The pleasure of taking things apart, understanding their workings and rebuilding them" was evident in his first commercial hit, *American Graffiti*, before Star Wars (Brooker 2020, 34). This love of hardware and the fun of interacting with it is part of what drives Star Wars stories. Organic non-people, like Chewbacca, also play with objects (like an odd welding tool for fixing the Millennium Falcon) and relate to humans in ways that feel simultaneously strange and familiar. R2-D2 and Chewbacca are like adored, loyal pets but also intelligent friends, annoying coworkers, and sometimes even tools—a single character might be two or even all of these things. Star Wars material characters collaborate with the fictional world they dwell within to constitute a concrete fictional environment characterized by what I call the *Star Wars thing aesthetic*. This aesthetic is a collection of qualities that describe the saga's attitude towards material objects. The *Star Wars thing aesthetic* is *extra-mundane*, *recycled*, *archeological*, *hybrid*, and *playful*. Each of these qualities supports a cohesive aesthetic that material characters help deliver.

I begin with the quality *extra-mundane*, because it is possibly the characteristic most commonly referred to by fans and Star Wars creators, what Grossman describes as "the quotidian made strange and beautiful, the terrestrial made alien" (Grossman 2015, 71), a two-way transformation between the dull and amazing. Star Wars characters take for granted a spaceship that travels at light speed, or a robot who speaks multiple languages—things we in the audience can only imagine. In his book *I Find Your Lack of Faith Disturbing: Star Wars and the Triumph of Geek Culture*, A.D. Jameson suggests that Star Wars characters in the first film were cleverly scripted with blasé attitudes towards the "miraculous technology surrounding them," which is part of how Star Wars "renders the remarkable mundane" (Jameson 2018, 34–5). He reminds us that when Luke Skywalker first meets R2 and C-3PO at the Jawas' droid sale, he "barely takes any notice of the duo. To him, they're just more chores" (Jameson 2018, 34). Audiences may have been engrossed by these high-tech robots and their mysterious captors, but the human inhabitants of Tatooine are unimpressed with this used equipment they are forced to settle for. Luke later responds with disgust when he first sees the Millennium Falcon, exclaiming "What a piece of junk!'" (Jameson 2018, 45)—never mind that it travels at light speed, which is impossible and amazing to we Earthlings. So much beauty and strangeness in the stuff of Star Wars is made extra-mundane in these interactions between the humans and the non-humans—even when there is affection and care in fixing, rescuing, or building.

Things do not go to waste in this galaxy. Star Wars cares for its stuff in part by forever repurposing it. Like the self-created droid L3-37 from *Solo,* the Star Wars thing aesthetic is *recycled.* Taking things and using them for renewed purposes is part of the fictional economy of survival in Star Wars; it's built-in. The Jawas churn and restart mechanical lives in the deserts of Tatooine—it is their business that brings droids to Luke Skywalker, setting the whole saga in motion. The hero of the sequels, Rey (Daisy Ridley), also scavenges for a living and lives inside the head of an abandoned Imperial Walker. The characters' junk orientation reflects the real-life creation of live-action Star Wars. Many of the props and set pieces in the original film, *Episode IV: A New Hope,* were amalgamations (both in terms of design and actual conceptual model construction) of repurposed real-world objects. Grossman writes that building the first Star Wars film in the 1970s involved scavenging for "interesting-looking spare parts from model kits and junkyards to make the ships and vehicles." His interview with Gary Tomkins, art director for *Episode VII: The Force Awakens* (and son of Alan Tomkins, art director for *Empire*), indicates how deep this recycling tradition goes. Forty-plus years later, Tomkins brings that same approach, describing how he searches for bits of abandoned industrial things and "likes to crack open washing machines and fridges and TVs in search of interesting shapes" (Grossman 2015, 70). This habit helps lend Star Wars what Grossman calls an "uncanny familiarity" and what creature effects supervisor Neal Scanlan describes as a "visual umbilical between the world that we're living in our everyday lives and the one we're watching on the screen" (Grossman 2015, 71). Pieces of our actual analog world help create some Star Wars material characters as well. The bounty hunter droid IG-88, a lesser-known side character who appears for barely a blink beside Boba Fett in *Empire,* was made from a Rolls Royce jet engine part used for, and then later salvaged from, the Mos Eisley cantina bar (Romano 2015). This droid's look was then recycled into IG-11, who played a more developed role as a bounty-hunter turned nursing droid in *The Mandalorian* several decades later.

The dirt, wear-and-tear, and general agedness of many Star War things suggests a hidden background, an intriguing history. The creators' tendencies to move back and forth in time (and to tickle fan nostalgia by bringing old things back) makes the Star Wars thing aesthetic *archeological.* Will Brooker writes about how R2's "carbon-scored bodywork, like Luke's battered speeder ... bear testament to previous adventures," which offers enticing blanks to fill in (Brooker 2020, 32). As Grossman writes about the original film, "The dirt gave everything an extra dimension, not of space but of time: the objects in the Star Wars universe had a history that stretched back before the start of the

FIGURE 1.1 The droid IG-11 from the first season of *The Mandalorian* (LUCASFILM)

movie" (Grossman 2015, 73). These scratches and marks can also make the objects more empathy-inducing, as if they are wounded. We might wonder what created those scars. What did that bounty hunter do to get that dent in his helmet?

The Star Wars thing aesthetic is also *hybrid*. Characters that are not droids are also not quite people, yet they seem to fit right in wherever they fall along this line. This is because its designers use the material in costumes and practical effects that combine the organic and inorganic, often blurring the line between creature and thing. Even the voices are part organic, part mechanic, per sound designer Ben Burtt's imaginative hybridizations. From the original trilogy forward, Burtt often used everyday objects to create unique sounds, and sometimes mixed them with recorded voices of humans and animals. He created R2-D2's voice, for example, by combining an ARP 2600 synthesizer sound with his own vocalizations (Schwartz 2021); part of his approach to combining manufactured sounds with what Jameson describes as a "gritty, 'organic' quality" (Jameson 2018, 38). There are hybrid Star Wars creatures: the Porgs from *Episode VIII: The Last Jedi* are "designed as a cross between a seal, a puffin and a pug dog" (Giardina 2018). Some humans look like droids and are partially made of machines. Seeing some material character types, you cannot tell on first view (or even the hundredth?) whether they are organic or mechanical, and it seems such distinctions are deliberately blurred. The Jawas' eyes look like they are made of electric red lights. And the Tuskens, first identified as Sand People, have human bodies, but their faces appear to be composed of cloth and metallic horns (they are actually masks, but that's not revealed in the films).

Above all, the Star Wars thing aesthetic is *playful*. Luke Skywalker in the first film has a brief, fleeting moment of flying a toy starship as he procrastinates his chores and whines about his life. Like many young adults with dreams, he longs to play with the real thing—and soon, he will. Characters playing with spaceships and light-up swords echo children moving action figures around at home, and the modelmakers exploding things at ILM. Star Wars helped make that a grown-up job. John Bell writes about how puppetry is "inextricably linked to long-standing desires to play with the material world" (Bell 2014, 43), and it is in this final quality of the thing aesthetic that we see its closest ties to the art of puppetry.

The Star Wars Material Character Journey

This section looks at the overall shape of material character participation over the course of 45+ years of live-action Star Wars, beginning with the original trilogy (1977–1983) and continuing up to the launching of the first live-action TV series of the early 2020s. Examining these films as groups in release order reveals how material characters proved their expansive capacities as meaning-makers, and how they evolved over time. This overview also provides a background and context to support detailed character analyses in the chapters to follow.

Original Trilogy (1977–1983)

Star Wars began in 1977 with two minutes and forty seconds of ships and robots. As *Atlantic* writer Spencer Kornhaber recalls, "The first act of the movie is mind-blowing in that there are almost no real, recognizable people in it … the frame fills with the masks of stormtroopers and Darth Vader, and with the metallic visages of R2-D2 and C-3PO," making it hard to determine who is human and who is machine in all the chaos (Kornhaber 2019). Then on Tatooine come the Jawas, the Tuskens, and all manner of strange barflies at the Mos Eisley cantina where we meet our first principal creature, a Wookiee named Chewbacca. Film critic Gary Arnold was particularly taken with the cantina and its "bubble-headed, long-snouted patrons" when he reviewed the film in 1977. He was one of the few critics to recognize the value of the non-humans in *Star Wars*, and he was impressed by the way Lucas presented them:

> These characters prove wonderfully amusing company in their own right, but their entrances are enhanced by a fantastic, hilarious setting—a futuristic cantina catering to all the human, semi-human and non-human riffraff in the territory …. Although the look of Star Wars has been influenced by Kubrick … the tone and tempo are utterly, happily different from "2001" or "A Clockwork Orange." Lucas' film is jaunty rather than portentous …. New perspectives and monsters keep turning up and moving on with astonishing and amusing rapidity. Lucas' style of sci-fi prodigality is playfully funny.
>
> *(Arnold 1977)*

These early Star Wars material characters established a certain tone, as Arnold suggests, which would help define future Star Wars world-building. The cantina customers also play a part in the hero's journey—a term popularized by writer Joseph Campbell, who has used Luke Skywalker to exemplify it. We witness in the cantina Luke's first attempt at civilized negotiations with strange characters in a new environment, and it doesn't go well—he's nearly killed at the bar within the first few minutes. This scene constitutes a step in Luke's growth from a dreamy adolescent to a heroic adult in the first film, and it puts him on a larger journey in his relationship with the non-human that *Empire* takes up as Luke grows into a Jedi. While the first film introduces the material characters, with all of their compelling and unusual characteristics, *Empire* elevates and deepens their importance, particularly in relation to the human hero. Luke Skywalker's confrontation with himself and the spiritual foundation of "the force," discovered in *Empire,* is shaped by material characters—in particular Yoda, who in 1980 inaugurated complexity in Star Wars puppet design and story function.

As the second film in the first trilogy, *Empire* also expanded creatures' and droids' functions and characteristics. There was a new bug-like "probe droid" that floated above the snow and offered the film's inciting incident by identifying the rebel base. *Empire* also introduced medical droids who tend to Luke's injuries at the beginning and the end of the film. One of the most whimsical types of material characters invented for *Empire* was a super-vibrant object, the Imperial Walker. These enormous tanks lumber on four legs and shoot blasters out of cheek cannons from head-shaped cockpits where a pilot (puppeteer?) drives them from within. More iterations of the Walker show up in subsequent films, some on two legs, some on four, always a bit more alive than any weapon should be.

Episode VI: Return of the Jedi made deeper use of the mask in 1983 with the tense archetypal father-son conflict between Luke and Vader, and there appeared to be an indulgence, even a celebration of so much material personality in the film. There were now more intelligent creatures, like the suit character Admiral Ackbar (Timothy D. Rose), who issues commands from his squid-shaped mouth, and a whole new society called Ewoks. The two droids are once again our guides, and the first series of scenes they bring us to in *Return of the Jedi* are so full of material characters they merit a more detailed description. The film opens with R2 and C-3PO back on the sands of Tatooine, entering Jabba's palace so that the audience encounters its inhabitants through their eyes. Even the doorbell to Jabba's palace is a puppet: a sphere juts out of a big metal door like a robot eyeball. We enter the palace to encounter the muscular, horned green Gamorrean guards along with Bib Fortuna (Michael Carter), a hairless humanoid with red eyes, and a head that twists into thick tendrils around his shoulders. Once we get into the palace's main chamber, we see a scene similar to the cantina of old, with musicians and dancers, and are given a glimpse of familiar characters from *Empire*, like the masked Boba Fett (Jeremy Bulloch). The scene finally reveals Jabba the Hutt himself, an enormous slug-like puppet on a moving throne. Beneath him is a dungeon where droids are tortured and conscripted into service. Princess Leia (Carrie Fisher) enters the scene disguised as a helmeted bounty hunter, but once caught, she ends up in the giant puppet Jabba's lap, dressed in a metal bikini and leashed by a chain. Luke arrives and is nearly eaten by a giant Rancor monster (performed by a small hand puppet made to appear enormous in the film) before he and his friends are taken to the desert to be fed to a puppet in the sand called the Sarlacc. Luke and friends stage an escape, while Leia single-handedly strangles Jabba with her chain. Most of the bad guys are killed or swallowed by the Sarlacc—a mouth-like creature recessed in a sandy pit—including Boba Fett. This battle is bookended by the film's finale, where a furry society of Ewoks join the rebels in scrappy guerilla-style warfare to defeat the Empire in the trilogy's triumphant ending. *Return of the Jedi*'s sheer volume of non-humans earned criticism at the time, but history would take the side of the puppet-lovers. Four decades later, Disney's successful streaming series would build on the very aesthetic established by the original trilogy—most especially *Jedi*—reviving those same material characters to make some of Star Wars' most successful live-action stories.

Prequels (1999–2005)

In the late 1990s, Lucasfilm launched a trilogy of films set a generation prior to the original trilogy. It tells the story of how young Anakin Skywalker grew up to become Darth Vader amidst the turmoil of political change and rising authoritarianism that would birth the Empire. There are more material characters in the prequels in part because George Lucas's special effects company, ILM, applied CGI on a mass scale to generate not only artificial sets, but multitudes of digitally animated creatures and droids. So with few exceptions (the naked-wire C-3PO puppet in *Phantom* for one), the CGI look dominates the material characters in this trilogy. Though the films were extremely successful at the box office, they were met with a great deal of disappointment and criticism by fans and reviewers. One of the biggest complaints was the flat, unappealing, and even offensive characterization of non-humans and semi-humans in particular.

The character Jar Jar Binks (Ahmed Best) is the most famous symbol for Lucas's mistakes in the prequels. Jar Jar's Wikipedia entry summarizes reactions this way: "He was met with overwhelming dislike from both critics and audiences, and is recognized as one of the most hated characters in Star Wars and the history of film in general" ("Jar Jar Binks," n.d.). Jar Jar's infamy contrasted notably with the extreme adoration shown to R2-D2, Chewbacca, and other material characters from the original trilogy, who remain popular to this day.

Like Yoda, Jar Jar was an experiment in pushing an existing technology further, yet Yoda is considered one of the most successful examples of creature effects in the history of film, while Jar Jar was named #1 in ABC News's "The Top 10 Worst TV and Film Characters" (Marikar 2010). The prequel's CGI figures and effects are often quite imaginative, even beautiful—CGI is responsible for the shimmering underwater creatures of Naboo, for example, and the iridescent dragon-like Varactyl Obi-Wan rides in *Episode III: Revenge of the Sith*—but the overall intermixing of the digital and real was unsuccessful as a live-action tool, particularly in *Phantom*, which established the new trilogy's aesthetic direction. Like the humans, the material characters traverse the ground and seem to obey gravity, at least superficially, but they often move in improbable ways—and they are bouncy, rather like video game characters. *Phantom* introduces Watto (voiced by Andy Secombe), a CGI slug-like creature about the size of a human toddler who is particularly problematic. For example, he has insect-like wings unlikely to support his body weight, which makes him simultaneously implausible and unrelatable as a being who exists in the same space as the humans he interacts with. That he, Jar Jar, and many other CGI creatures from the prequels also perform racial stereotypes is a problem I investigate in Chapter 5.

The prequel trilogy did improve its use of CGI in some ways over the course of the three films, strengthening the contribution of this type of material character. While the lack of physical restraint on an animated image can make characters less plausible, as with Watto, CGI's unique qualities can work well in live-action when their qualities and limitations are well-employed. *Episode II: Attack of the Clones* (2002) and *Episode III: Revenge of the Sith* (2005) feature three groups of material characters whose engagement with CGI (and one another) creates meaning: the non-human Kaminoans, the semi-human clones in the Kaminoan factory, and a concealed human Jango Fett. Introduced in *Attack of the Clones*, the Kaminoans are elegant, ghostly-looking creatures living on a planet made of rainstorms. These skinny, rabbit-faced animated figures seem to glow by nature. They are bipedal, but rather than walk like people, they glide. Their look and movement turns CGI limitations into beneficial characteristics, using what I call the duality of limited limitlessness (which we'll explore in Chapter 2). Cloners by trade, the Kaminoans are growing thousands of soldiers from fetuses to fully mature men, genetically engineered for obedience and trained to fight. When Obi-Wan Kenobi (Ewan McGregor) arrives on Kamino, his hosts give him a tour of their sleek workplace, gesturing this way and that with their long, fluid hands, pointing proudly around their booming person-factory. The Kaminoans run a manufacturing facility whose assembly lines of semi-humans also make thoughtful use of CGI's affordances. Mass duplication is an easier task for the computer-generated image than the practical character; and that tool had already been deployed in *Phantom*, where a mass droid army and crowds that go on forever help tell the story on the visual scale Lucas envisioned. But miles of identical robots are only so interesting;

manufactured babies and men who all move differently but look the same—that is something else indeed, and it's a perfect job for CGI. Because of the digital technology, the faces of actors Daniel Logan (the child generation, who look like a young Boba Fett) and Temuera Morrison (the adult generation, who look like Jango Fett) could be multiplied by the hundreds. Those faces are later hidden under helmet-masks when they become the clone troopers in *Episode III: Revenge of the Sith*. While Jango Fett's own mask and armor differ from the clones', his occasional concealment offers a reminder that the face beneath—indeed his whole person—is being duplicated.

The material character approach in the prequels was not all about CGI; there were a number of other creative choices that advanced the story with objects. Chief among these was the use of Vader's mask in the climax of the final film, *Revenge of the Sith*. But by and large, the shift towards a mostly digital approach to material characters dominated this trilogy. The non-human, semi-human, and concealed human character could now be an image instead of, as well as, or in combination with, the practical material figure.

Sequel Trilogy (2015–2019)

The sequel films, produced after Disney acquired Lucasfilm, would pick up the plot of the original trilogies several decades later—telling the story of a now middle-aged Luke, Leia, and Han (Harrison Ford), and the son of the latter two, Kylo Ren (Adam Driver), the new villain. Its new human heroes, Rey and Finn (John Boyega), would interact with more tangible physical environments as well as old-school puppeteered creatures and droids. While the prequels didn't entirely depart from elements of the Star Wars thing aesthetic, the sequels leaned into it much more. The film introduces Rey as a masked scavenger who survives by repurposing select things (some of which she keeps as toys), and then fixing and selling other bits of metal stuff pulled out of larger found objects. She cleans and prepares her finds in the desert of the planet Jakku among metal-faced humanoids and hairy or loose-skinned beasts of burden of all shapes and sizes lumbering in and out of frame. It is her attachment to the droid BB-8 that draws Rey into the galaxy's adventures. This film also introduces new expansions on the helmet-mask: a super-vibrant object in Darth Vader's burned helmet-face, a new masked villain in Kylo Ren, and a new take on stormtroopers (in the characters Finn and Phasma)—all of which take advantage of the qualities of material characters.

The sequel trilogy didn't switch back to the original reliance on practical material characters entirely, however, but seems to have discovered a balance between the tangible and digital. The films found a way to ground the CGI characters in an actor-driven way. The diminutive Maz Kanata (Lupita Nyong'o) and the eerie uber-villain, Snoke (Andy Serkis), both came to life via performance-capture CGI, enabling a more intimate collaboration between the actor and image. But just as digital technology could now do more to include the presence of the human in this interactive way, it has also been employed to seamlessly erase a puppeteer's image, and thereby expand the parameters of how a material character can be designed and performed. For example, the droid BB-8 was sometimes puppeteered in action sequences that likely benefitted from choices made by performers Dave Chapman or Brian Herring. Unlike the pre-CGI material characters of old, neither Chapman nor Herring had to hide (as Frank Oz did beneath the floors of Yoda's house), because their images could be eliminated in post-production. The big-eyed, pigeon-like Porgs in *The Last Jedi* came to life via a combination of CGI, animatronics, and multiple puppetry rods moved by four or five puppeteers at a time (Giardina 2018). As is frequently the case in live theatre, the puppeteers in these examples were rendered invisible in order to make a material character appear magically alive. Many of the sequel trilogy's characters combined digital and practical effects in this and other ways, and the differences between the two approaches have grown increasingly indistinct over time.

The second film, *Episode VIII: The Last Jedi,* brought a wide array of whimsical beings to Star Wars in 2017. The aged Luke, once again a man among creatures, lives on the isle of Lanai, where he milks the many teats of enormous Thala-sirens for his blue liquid breakfast, and dwells peaceably alongside the quietly hardworking Lanai caretakers—short humanoids, dressed a bit like nuns, with turtle-like faces. When Chewbacca visits the island, he cooks one of the Porgs for food, but ends up befriending the creatures, who later build nests in the Millennium Falcon like urban birds. There is an elegant moment in *The Last Jedi* that contrasts with the unsuccessful buffoonery of the preceding prequel trilogy—showing a simpler, more grounded approach to material character humor. Rey is practicing her lightsaber moves on top of a hill on the island when she accidentally slices a boulder in two. The top half of the rock plummets down the hill, ramming into splinters the cart that a pair of Lanai are pushing along. The two freeze for a moment, staring into the vacant air where their cart just was, holding onto the now-useless handles. After the perfect length of a pause, the two faces glance up at Rey. This funny, speechless moment demonstrates the simple pause-and-gaze language masks and puppets use in physical theatre. *The Last Jedi* also brings Yoda back full circle from his prequel days as a CGI character to the puppet he once was for an intimate scene between the aged Luke and his old master (now a Force ghost, but it hardly matters; there is so much "there" there in Frank Oz's return to puppeteering and voicing this practical character). There is also an interesting puppet-oriented epilogue to the film where a group of children make a story of a homemade Luke doll facing down an Imperial Walker, echoing the way fans play with miniaturized versions of the story characters (i.e., action figures).

The final film, *The Rise of Skywalker*, is outright self-referential about its puppetry—almost to a startling degree. The digital character Maz Kanata returns as a practical puppet. Snoke's body parts are displayed in multiple spec-imen jars, revealing him to have been a fake, manipulated by the reanimated emperor (the great puppet master of Snoke and so much else). There is literally a puppet show about twenty minutes into the film, entertaining children at a festival much like they do on Earth. But even more interesting is how this final film seems to want its material characters to be awkward. Little Babu Frik (voiced by Shirley Henderson) is an animatronic puppet whose jerky arms and mouth recall figures from Disney amusement parks. He did not need to be thus—CGI or even another style of practical puppetry might have made him smoother—but his obvious puppet-ness lends him a certain charm and mate-rial assertiveness. *The Rise of Skywalker*'s embrace of awkwardness is an inter-esting cap to a trilogy committed to old-school tangibility in a digital age.

Between the trilogy films, Lucasfilm released two standalone stories of adventures and backstories inspired by the original trilogies, *Rogue One* (2016) and *Solo* (2018). Both featured a new type of droid that broke prior molds in terms of both their place in the story and the approach to performance. In *Rogue One*, the imposing K-2SO (Alan Tudyk) is brought to life with the same caliber of comic virtuosity as C-3PO, but Tudyk's approach is drier and more sar-casm-laden. Because he is not silly like C-3PO, nor adorable like R2-D2, K-2SO expanded on what droid characters can be beyond those now-established types, while still capitalizing on what makes them so effective. The primary droid character in *Solo*, a female(!) named L3-37 (Phoebe Waller-Bridge), is Star Wars' most self-referential droid. Unlike the reflective but content C-3PO, L-3 was written to challenge her dual nature as an intelligent thing, both alive and not.

Live-Action Streaming Series (2019–)

At this writing, Disney is continuing to create one live-action Star Wars streaming series after another. Each is similar to a long film, and their stories are interconnected but tend (so far) to focus on events that take place before the sequel films, in terms of timeline. The first two series, *The Mandalorian* (2019–) and *The Book of Boba Fett* (2021–2022) represent a precedent-setting pattern of foregrounding and expanding the role of material characters.

The first season of *The Mandalorian* unfolds in eight episodes with subplots that surround a central throughline for the helmet-mask protagonist and his relationship with a tiny green creature who looks like a baby version of Yoda. Fans called the little one "Baby Yoda," and in 2019 this animatronic/rod pup-pet quickly entered the canon of most beloved Star Wars characters. These series have put material characters at the center of action for the first time in live-action Star Wars history. They also take interest in side-character stories from the original trilogy. Dave Filoni and Jon Favreau, producers working on the early streaming series, seemed to be attuned to the playfulness of the

Star Wars thing aesthetic in their inspiration. Both referred to their own childhood memories of playing with secondary characters—and what they imagined about them. Filoni explained it this way when the two were interviewed for *Entertainment Weekly:* "These are the [action figures] you got. Your older brothers have had 'good' ones. Somehow you got Boba Fett. And if you have Boba Fett, you could always tell a good story." Favreau described his inspiration this way: "I've always been curious what the other people in the cantina are up to …. We're digging really deep in the toy chest and pulling out the action figures that people were always curious about and were not quite in the center frame, but have a lot of potential" (Hibberd 2019). This speaks to the playfulness of Star Wars and the power of its material characters, whether in center frame or—perhaps more enticingly—barely in view. And perhaps what the first Star Wars film team initially included in the films as tools of atmospheric world-building were, with the passage of time, more likely than the humans to impact the viewer's memory. These odd beings, as Gary Arnold suggested of the cantina bar patrons, "leave some tantalizing unanswered questions about Tatooine civilization" (Arnold 1977), which the new Star Wars creators, now kids grown up, are endeavoring to answer with new stories.

Conclusion

In 1977, George Lucas and his team made a film that would establish a way of working with objects, environments, and creatures that I call the *Star Wars thing aesthetic* and characterize as extra-mundane, recycled, archeological, hybrid, and playful. This aesthetic relies on material characters and helped shape their evolution over 45+ years of live-action Star Wars. Reviewing how material characters grew and changed over the course of eleven feature films and two streaming series from 1977 to 2022, it's increasingly evident how critical material characters are to the franchise. As the films journeyed from a heavy reliance on practical effects (original trilogies) to CGI (prequels), to evolving combinations of the two (sequels and streaming series), they demonstrated their range of possible forms, intersections, and need for balance in a fictional galaxy where humans, creatures, and talking things coexist and communicate backwards and forwards across time and space. Now that we are oriented to this view of live-action Star Wars, the next chapters will analyze how creatures, droids, and masked people make meaning within the stories, and what that reveals about material character powers.

References

Arnold, Gary. 1977. "'Star Wars' (PG)." *The Washington Post*, May 25, 1977. https://www.washingtonpost.com/wp-srv/style/longterm/movies/review97/starwarsarnold.htm.

Bell, John. 2014. "Playing with the Eternal Uncanny: The Persistent Life of Lifeless Objects." In *The Routledge Companion to Puppetry and Material Performance*, edited by Claudia Orenstein, Dassia N. Posner, and John Bell. New York, NY: Routledge.

Brooker, Will. 2020. *Star Wars*. London: Bloomsbury Academic.

Giardina, Carolyn. 2018. "How 'Last Jedi' Used Real-World Animals to Create CG Porgs." *The Hollywood Reporter*, January 3, 2018. https://www.hollywoodreporter.com/movies/movie-news/how-last-jedi-used-real-world-animals-create-cg-porgs-1071139/.

Grossman, Lev. 2015. "A New Hope: How J.J. Abrams Brought Back Star Wars Using Puppets, Greebles and Yak Hair." *TIME Magazine*, December 14, 2015, 56–75.

Hibberd, James. 2019. "'The Mandalorian' Unmasked: 'We Did Things No "Star Wars" Fan Has Ever Seen.'" *Entertainment Weekly*, September 5, 2019. https://ew.com/tv/2019/09/05/inside-the-mandalorian-star-wars/.

Jameson, A.D. 2018. *I Find Your Lack of Faith Disturbing: Star Wars and the Triumph of Geek Culture*. New York, NY: Farrar, Straus and Giroux.

Kornhaber, Spencer. 2019. "'The Mandalorian' Season Finale Scrambles Man and Machine." *The Atlantic*, December 30, 2019. https://www.theatlantic.com/entertainment/archive/2019/12/mandalorian-season-finale-scrambles-man-and-machine/604237/.

Marikar, Sheila. 2010. "The Top 10 Worst TV and Film Characters." *ABC News*. https://abcnews.go.com/Entertainment/Movies/top-10-worst-tv-film-characters-time/story?id=10809609.

Romano, Steven. 2015. "5 Recycled Star Wars Props and Costumes." *StarWars.com*. https://web.archive.org/web/20190909213609/https://www.starwars.com/news/5-recycled-star-wars-props-and-costumes.

Schwartz, Gregory. 2021. "Ben Burtt, R2D2, and the Humanization of Synthesis in Sound Design." *Hii Magazine*. https://hii-mag.com/article/benburttr2d2.

Wikipedia, The Free Encyclopedia, s.v. "Jar Jar Binks." n.d. (Accessed November 5, 2022). https://en.wikipedia.org/wiki/Jar_Jar_Binks#cite_note-1.

2

DISTANCE, DISTILLATION, AND DUALITY

The Three Material Character Powers

In this chapter, I use Star Wars creatures, droids, and masked figures to demonstrate three powers of the material character: distance, distillation, and duality. *Distance* is the literal and figurative gap between the material character and the human. *Distillation* is the material character's special ability to perform concentrated ideas. *Duality* is their power to be at least two things at once, often paradoxes offering narrative opportunities both within and beyond the fiction. This trio of terms emerges from, builds upon, and simplifies analysis from contemporary puppet theatre scholars. Though I use a popular film series to explain them, these powers are applicable across all media, wherever material characters dwell. These three potencies intersect a great deal, but teasing them out—and using recognizable characters to demonstrate how they work—will illuminate how they create meaning.

Distance

Distance emerges in the way a character created by a puppet, suit, mask, or other practical/digital material is one or more degrees away from the exposed human. I centralize the human not to suggest the supremacy of our species, but to reflect the fact that from a performance perspective, it is actors (at this time, homo sapiens only) who portray characters in plays, films, etc., so bringing material into the picture automatically creates a certain distance. Semi-humans are intriguingly liminal: the unusual physical features of characters like Snoke or Ahsoka suggest they are both similar to and slightly apart from, for example, Leia or Luke. A concealed character wearing a helmet-mask (Darth Vader, Boba Fett) we may assume to be human, but their obscured face holds them at a certain remove. Not only is their facial identity compromised

DOI: 10.4324/9781003137559-3

(can we fully trust they are who they say they are?) but so is the audience's ability to fully interpret what they may be thinking or feeling. The mask creates a barrier, inhibiting the expression of humanness by a degree.

Distance is the primary power all material characters hold, and while it enables distillation and duality, it also has its own specific offerings. Distance offers broad choices in a character's shape and speech, the opportunity for a character to separate from itself, and the facilitation of violence.

Shape and Speech

Released from the constraints of the human form, a material character can be as large as a star, as tiny as a mosquito, and have as many eyes as you like. So there is a wide-open invitation to imagine into being a range of impossible or strange scales and abilities for creatures and animate things. Distance from the human also means that a character can be manifested in different ways in a single episode, or even a single scene because it invites composite possibilities. Darth Vader's original trilogy performance was created by a combination of several artists' efforts: the formidable physicality of the suit performance (bodybuilder David Prowse), skilled swordplay (fight expert Bob Anderson), a mechanical breathing sound (designed by Brett Burr), and deeply textured voice acting (actor James Earl Jones). Distance both calls upon and enables such an impossible being as Darth Vader through his status as a material character.

Animated characters rendered in computer-generated imagery (CGI) have the flexible capacity to toy with extremes in appearance. They need not be aligned with the anatomy of the human body in the way the suit character must, nor wrestle with the weight and other physical attributes of a practical puppet, so they can be highly flexible and wide-ranging in design and movement.

The distance from the human not only invites imaginative solutions to how a material character can look and move, but how they might speak. We take for granted that in the human body, the voice is fluid: people utter sounds with their vocal cords and shape them with their mouths, then make facial movements and hand gestures—all of which is executed and interpreted without a lot of conscious thought. With a practical material character, there is an implicit invitation to create an alternative way of communicating born of necessity: they cannot speak like people because they have no vocal cords and cannot shape sound into speech the way we do. As Kenneth Gross writes in *Puppet: An Essay on Uncanny Life*, "the puppet's voice always comes from the outside. Its voice is always alien, never its own" (Gross 2011, 67). The full-face mask on a performer—in Star Wars, the helmet-mask character—obscures the mouth and replaces it with something hard and unmoving. This is also an opportunity for a wide range of different types of voices: a masked hard-faced material character like C-3PO can "speak" via voiceover to give the indication of almost any type of clear speech coming from behind that fixed, expression-less visage. Anthony Daniels voices the droid he physically performs, as is the case with many helmet-masked characters like Boba Fett, but a division between body and voice can also be an advantageous choice, as with the voice of Darth Vader, which feels eerily removed from the villain's helmet-face and loud, mechanical breathing. A material character's voice is often designed for a particular personality or effect. In Star Wars, a droid might speak in mechanical beeps; a creature can utter a made-up language that might sound more like an animal than a human. Chewbacca's voice, for example, is a combination of animal sound recordings that include a walrus and a bear (Salisbury 2018, 29). Droids and creatures might require translation, which can intensify their interdependence with another character. We learn what Chewbacca is saying through Han's reactions; C-3PO's one-sided translations of R2's emotional tones are part of the duo's comic vernacular. C-3PO was one of the few original material characters designed to talk like a human, but his inflexible mechanical face—with only a rectangular, unmoving slit for a mouth—also helps shape the character. The fact that he cannot accompany his human voice with the kind of fluid facial expressions a person might necessitates more gestural language. And the discordant intersection between C-3PO's proper English speech and unmoving mouth underscore his ironic, humorous distance from the humans he's trying to simultaneously imitate, instruct, and serve.

CGI characters can move their mouths fluidly like humans or animals, creating the illusion of that unity of sound and expression that is often more challenging for a practical puppet. But CGI can also give these virtual figures a cartoonish appearance when conversing with humans—so that where there is unity within their own image as a character, they don't seem to belong in the live-action society around them, making them less believable. Performance capture CGI, however, counters that problem by connecting the artificial face to a real one. Maz Kanata, for example, can communicate linguistically in more detail because her face is tracked via motion capture technology to correspond with actress Lupita Nyong'o's.

Separation

Some puppets, suits, and masks are composed of a material item holding integrity of its own when removed from the human actor. In Star Wars, creators often take advantage of the way helmet-mask characters can move in and out of material character status by donning or removing the helmet. The fact that Vader's mask could be separated from or placed onto a human drives the tension of the original trilogy storyline, and propels the dramatic question of the prequels. The ability to oscillate between the human and material character, via the helmet-mask, has invited more incidental opportunities for storytelling in scenes within some of the films as well. Luke and Han escape capture inside the Death Star in *Episode IV: A New Hope* by putting on stormtrooper masks and armor; then Luke surprises Princess Leia when they first meet and he removes the helmet to declare himself her rescuer. Leia enters *Episode VI: Return of the Jedi* impersonating a bounty hunter who speaks in a strange, scratchy voice and alien tongue through the helmet-mask. Presumably, even the 1980s audience did not know it was Leia until she removed the mask to reveal herself and give Han a kiss.

The mask's connection to its human host in Star Wars can remain evocative when removed, lending it agency to impact those around it when there is no one inside. In *Episode II: Attack of the Clones*, the young Boba Fett mourns the death of Jango Fett by reverently holding his father's helmet up to his face. Possession of Jango/Boba's iconic mask later becomes a point of conflict and intrigue—as it changes heads and becomes a sought-after object—in *The Book of Boba Fett* streaming series.

Violence

Distance from humans enables material characters to enact and withstand violence in practical and meaningful ways. According to Eileen Blumenthal's *Puppetry: A World History*, puppets are tortured, decapitated, disembodied, pierced, strangled, and otherwise quite brutally and creatively abused and killed—very, very often, and have been since the dawn of play all over the world (Blumenthal 2005, 144). In her chapter on the subject of puppet violence, she suggests that "knowing that the performers are not alive, audiences do not activate emotional defenses, the mental filters that screen out or distance what would be unbearable to see" (Blumenthal 2005, 144). Victoria Nelson notes in her book *The Secret Life of Puppets* how popular Anglo-American cinema of the mid-twentieth century ushered in a wave of killer robots and demonic dolls (Nelson 2003, 258), which depended on material characters. But live-action Star Wars remains, as Lucas intended, a family-friendly series. This is enabled by the way material characters, who are ontologically distanced both in material and meaning, bear the brunt of the violence necessary for Star Wars action. Jawas, Stormtroopers, everyone in Jabba's palace—they're all treated as dispensable. There are some scenes of human torture, but it's usually before or after the fact, just a glimpse to let us know what's happening and leaving the rest to audience imagination. In contrast, in *Return of the Jedi,* a whole chamber is reserved for full-view droid torture (executed by another droid, apparently in charge of routine punishment). This is not to say that humans don't suffer violence in Star Wars, they sometimes do; significantly, *Rogue One* breaks the pattern by ending with the death of its two protagonists. But it is an unquestionable function of the material characters in Star Wars in general to tell the story of war casualties with comparatively low loss of human life. There are some gruesome acts, but these are reserved for "aliens" and robots, such as the droid who is unceremoniously run over by Han's speeder in *Solo*. In *The Rise of Skywalker*, Kylo Ren dumps the severed head of a horned humanoid named Boolio (Aidan Cook) on a conference table for effect—no doubt meant to be a *little* gross and horrifying, but less so than if it were a person, certainly. The briefly-seen Boolio is voice-acted by Mark Hamill, and one can only imagine if Hamill's human character, Luke Skywalker, ended up decapitated. To be fair, Luke's face *is* separated from his body during his vision of its appearance in Darth Vader's mask in *Empire*, but that is a terrifying dream moment, with just the right amount of horror, and was itself a powerful material character scene.

Death and injury of the helmet-masks is depersonalized because not only is there no blood to clean up when these characters are abused, we don't really see them because they have no faces and all look the same. And, of course, concealment serves to dampen empathy that might be inspired by beholding a human face. Stormtroopers are dispensable bad guys, but they aren't even *guys*, really, at all. A step or two away from the human in this fictional world, Star Wars material characters can withstand a range of violence played upon their bodies, which is practical for a story about war aimed at families, but it also carries its own meaning. The material character distance not only enables a kind of halfway point to approach horror through its obscured representation, but it also allows us to consider violence more abstractly. For example, *The Mandalorian* and *The Book of Boba Fett* feature scenes of stormtrooper helmets impaled on stakes in the desert. These helmets look like skulls and are meant to—Lucas had wanted stormtroopers to have a skeletal look, hence the white-on-black design (*WIRED* 2022). And yet it's very important that these masks are not actual bones. The distance in meaning between the two materials—an artificial helmet, and an organic human skull—makes this image of impaled trooper masks both potent and palatable (similarly, distance enables young Boba Fett in *Attack of the Clones* to grieve over his father's empty helmet-mask, rather than his severed head). Stormtrooper helmets also slosh around the watery ruins of the Death Star in *Episode IX: The Rise of Skywalker*, presumably less to represent individual victims of war than the end of the power structure they served, the impotence of those terrorizing figures, and their defeat. The possibility of individual identities, what their faces might have looked like in suffering, and even the horror of war itself is simultaneously symbolized and blunted by the mask.

There is, in many ways, more self-reflection about the way masks represent humanity in post-Lucas live-action Star Wars. Premiered in 2015, *Episode VII: The Force Awakens* unexpectedly turns to focus on a stormtrooper's humanity after his mask is marked with the blood of his dying comrade. There is also a stack of Mandalorian helmets in *The Mandalorian*—a devastating visual statement about a recent genocidal act that the hero is spared witnessing. The audience is spared as well, which holds the tone of this series at the edge of seriousness, for better or worse, but the story does treat these particular helmets much more reverently. The dead are mourned by their survivors, if briefly, and their helmets are melted down (recycled and repurposed) to forge new armor for living Mandalorians to continue on.

Material characters' distance from humans enables violence in physical comedy as well. Blumenthal writes, "A great deal of puppet violence is more playful than serious." She offers farcical examples, from fights in Balinese *wayang* theatre (one featuring a comical decapitation) to Jim and Jane Henson's mid-century American TV commercials that reliably ended in violent puppet demise—these being the predecessors to the Muppets (Blumenthal 2005, 144), who are forever crashing into things and flying out of cannons. Star Wars material character violence is often more amusing than tragic. There are many examples of one material character eating other creatures in creative ways. For example, in *Return of the Jedi*, the Sarlacc swallows people and creatures whole, then (as explained with a straight face by C-3PO) digests them for a thousand years. A giant space worm temporarily ingests the Millennium Falcon in *Empire*, and the Krayt dragon eats elephant-size Banthas made comparatively ant-like in *The Mandalorian* (also examples of distance enabling extremes in scale).

There is also a great deal of limb dismemberment in Star Wars, which is never quite as horrific as it would be with full-stop human characters (I say "almost" because when audiences saw Vader slice off Luke's arm in the climax of *Empire* in 1980, it was exactly as shocking as it needed to be). A character like C-3PO, who may have feelings but is a machine without nerve endings, gets dismembered a good bit in live-action Star Wars in ways that are both comically clever and helpful to setting a balance in tone during violent action scenes. *The Empire Strikes Back* offers an excellent example; this film explodes the droid fully, then puts him back together in a way that is funny, alarming, and unique to material characters. The action takes place in Cloud City, where C-3PO wanders into a side room, then shortly finds himself blown to pieces. When a concerned Chewbacca goes searching, he discovers a room full of droid parts and a conveyor belt reminiscent of a trash processor, manned by a group of humanoid Ugnaughts (suit characters) who tease Chewbacca by playing keep away with C-3PO's head. Chewbacca eventually manages to collect all of the pieces of his companion into a single box, which he later unpacks in his prison cell in an attempt to reassemble his friend. This requires some experimental tinkering, which results in C-3PO's head successfully affixed, but—oops—when he turns on the lights in the droid's eyes, thus reviving his consciousness, he discovers he's on backwards! C-3PO scolds his rescuer, but there isn't time to correct the mistake. As they join their friends to blast their way out of Cloud City, C-3PO ends up riding around in a sack on Chewbacca's back, facing the wrong way. His disconnected limbs jostle as he comments on the battle scenes, providing comic relief throughout these action sequences in ways that only a material character can. This kind of performance is possible in ways that are obvious but important to unpack: C-3PO is not one and the same flesh as the actor who plays him—unlike Billy Dee Williams, for example, who shares face and body with Lando Calrissian. This distance between the actor and character enables these scenes in a practical sense, of course: C-3PO can survive decapitation and live on in pieces because he can be easily fixed; he is less vulnerable. This fact will be exploited again later in the prequels, where his head and body are separated and attached to a battle droid in a comical mismatch. Because C-3PO is humanoid but not human—and also, importantly, because he presumably cannot feel pain—he is a step or two away from the "us" that is Daniels and all other humans, and therefore the droid's mutilation and imperfect re-assemblage is comical rather than grotesque.

Distance is a power all material characters wield as non-, semi-, or concealed humans. It enables them to play with shape and speech, separation, and violence. Distance also enables two other broad powers of distillation and duality.

Distillation

Distillation is the material character's ability to perform concentrated ideas. Puppetry scholars have a range of expressions for this concept and its implications. Penny Francis calls the puppet a "representation and distillation of a character" (Francis 2012, 13). Claudia Orenstein describes puppets as "bearers of precise visual meaning" (Orenstein 2014, 4). Puppeteer Eric Bass suggests that the puppet's appearance is itself the language they bring to a story. He shares recalling Big Bird co-creator Kermit Love's view that "when an actor comes onstage, he needs to make a statement; when the puppet comes onstage, it IS the statement" (Bass 2014, 55). That visual meaning, that pared-down or bold statement the material character makes is immediately implied because they are designed and performed to communicate a specific idea.

Jabba the Hutt's 1983 appearance in *Return of the Jedi* is one of the best examples of how distillation works in Star Wars material characters. Conceived as a fearsome, elusive crime boss, Jabba was first performed by a human being in the original 1977 *Star Wars*. But the scene—like many featuring secondary human characters—didn't make the final cut. So after six years of hearing about him, the original audiences finally beheld Jabba's royal person in 1983's *Episode VI: Return of the Jedi*. For Jabba's premiere before audiences, this creature was a "design free-for-all" according to creature designer Phil Tippett, and at least one design suggestion was rejected by Lucas as "too human" (Salisbury 51). Jabba was ultimately created as a puppet—a huge, wide-mouthed, snake-eyed mound of rubber and drool, performed by multiple puppeteers (including Toby Philpott, Mike Edmonds, and David Barclay). The Jabba we behold in

FIGURE 2.1 Jabba the Hutt in *Return of the Jedi* (LUCASFILM)

Jedi is therefore not a man with double chins: rather, Jabba *is* a double chin, a material manifestation of a caricature. As an allegory for gluttonous greed, the puppet is an exaggerated embodiment of distilled characteristics associated with the sleazy crime-boss archetype. Metaphors assert themselves as whole when performed as a concrete physical image: Jabba likes to throw his weight around, literally.

Of course, human characters can be hyperbolic as well, but the material character's ability to exaggerate in movement, sound, and visual design is much broader; because they are made-up beings, they can dig deeper into their expression of whatever idea it is their job to convey. Also, they tend to rely less (and often not at all) on human psychology. Because of this distillation, material characters can be particularly effective at communicating bold characteristics, then upending expectations. If material characters like Yoda and Vader do eventually break the mold of what they are materially designed to be and express (and Vader does, literally), it can be quite compelling to witness.

The distillation embedded into the material character's design can then be reinforced by the character's performance. The first thing many puppeteers are taught is that the puppet must appear as if they are breathing. This is a distillation of life down to its essence: the breath, the thing that divides the living from the non-living. Performing with figures like the puppet and mask also relies on stillness, pause, simple head turns, gaze, and gesture for communicating thought. The late puppeteer Nikki Tilroe, a trainer and coach for many years at the Eugene O'Neill Theater Center's National Puppetry Conference, where I had the opportunity to learn from her in the early 2000s, taught students how to puppeteer via gestures and pauses—starting and stopping in a movement phrase. We were tasked to use breath, and the sound of breath, almost like a kind of code. The idea is that the onlooker reads the sounds (or lack of sound) and sequencing of gaze, stillness, and movement to interpret a puppet's thoughts, intentions, and reactions. Puppeteer Basil Jones (of the renowned Handspring Puppet Company) has similarly described how puppets communicate in a kind of visual language, and how *War Horse* audiences hunger to interpret horse bows and ear twitches (Jones 2014, 65). Star Wars viewers are in a similar position, reading the way Baby Yoda moves his ears down when he's scared, R2-D2 rocks back and forth when excited, or Chewbacca throws his head back when pained.

Sound can be the distilled version of a voice for the Star Wars material character. In his 2016 book *The World According to Star Wars,* Cass Sunstein shares that in an early version of the first *Star Wars* script, R2-D2 had human speech (Sunstein 2016, 17), before he was pared down into the non-humanoid droid with a limited range of rich and expressive beeps combined with simple head turns to communicate. As Gary Arnold first described in 1977, he "has a 'vocabulary' of beeps and whistles, rather like Harpo Marx, and employs them to similar humorous effect" (Arnold 1977). We see this kind of expressive vernacular decades later in Grogu (Baby Yoda), who speaks in grunts and coos.

Distillation is embedded in the act of making a non-human character execute everyday actions, which can be deeply meaningful. As a made-up being, there is always a struggle for a material character to pretend to perform the simplest tasks—the act of puppeteering them is itself a distillation in their actions. As Basil Jones puts it:

> minor quotidian functions, like getting out of bed in the morning, or reaching for a cup just beyond one's grasp … can take on epic proportions for many observers when performed by a puppet. Audiences identify with this and feel a resonance with their own interaction with the word. The puppet, therefore, becomes the manifest incarnation of our own struggle to live, to be human, to act.
>
> (Jones 2014, 63)

Audiences watched Yoda's little puppet hands operate a cane and make stew before he held them up to lift a spaceship with the force in *Empire*. In *The Mandalorian*, the repaired IG-11 struggles to grasp a cup, to pick up and move a simple box, as his rescuer helps him re-learn the activities of daily life. These are deeply human, consequential activities expressed by the distillation of the material character.

Distillation is natural to the performing object, whether it be a puppet, mask, or other type of material character. Their ability to perform concentrated ideas is a result of being both crafted and animated for a particular purpose. Distillation might make a material character bold or hyperbolic, but it can also render them simply riveting in what Basil Jones calls the "performance of life" (Jones 2014, 61).

Duality

Material characters are almost always at least two things at once—and those things are often opposites. Australian puppetry scholar Margaret Williams writes, "Paradox seems inherent in the very concept of a living object, and playing with paradox is half the fun of puppet theory" (Williams 2007, 122). Dassia Posner illuminates the rather staggering scope of dualistic possibilities in her introduction to *The Routledge Companion to Puppetry and Material Performance*'s section on new forms of hybridizations in puppetry. The art form, she writes,

> assumes a kind of imaginative flexibility—even mental acrobatics—on the part of its viewers. The puppet is concomitantly alive and dead, serious and ironic, adult and childlike, mechanical and spontaneous, enthralling and uncanny. It is uniquely adept at simultaneity and fragmentation. Its voice can be separated from its body without generating confusion. It can be rent into pieces without the audience fearing for its life or soul.
>
> *(Posner 2014, 225)*

I suggest we collectively regard these and other juxtapositional qualities as dualities of the material character. By duality, I am talking about the ability to be both *this* and *that* incongruous thing. Material characters wield power to express multiple paradoxes, and some of the most enticing are those described here and elsewhere by Posner and other scholars investigating puppetry and material performance. In my efforts to simplify what all material characters can offer, I find most helpful and comprehensive these five dualities: novel familiarity, absent presence, limited limitlessness, living death, and real-fiction.

Novel Familiarity

When we see a material character, we often recognize in them something familiar combined with something new, or a thing known to us but presented in a novel way. Any newly created material character is novel, but the design and execution can also evoke things we see in our own world: the placement of eyes, or the way a head moves to indicate thought. Material familiarity can be ambiguous and potentially more literal if a character is built of stuff that's had a prior life—examples might be wood, leather, or animal hair (some of Chewbacca's fur comes from a yak). In the case of Star Wars, sometimes that familiarity might come from the tendency to recycle bits of our world. There is a style of theatre called found-object puppetry that features everyday items in performance—rolls of toilet paper, umbrellas, or plastic bags can all become characters if puppeteered convincingly. Part of the appeal of this type of theatre is that novel familiarity of items from our world used in unexpected ways and forming characters. The Star Wars thing aesthetic draws on a similar duality of a thing known and new in order to suggest its own expansiveness. Will Brooker calls this quality, what Lucas imagined as he planned the first film, "familiarity tinged with strangeness" (Brooker 2020, 30).

Even figures made of newly created, unfamiliar material, and/or intangible images (as with CGI animations), carry something we recognize. For example, a critter may have seven purple eyes, but they are eyes nonetheless. Of course, any newly introduced human character is a bit novel and always familiar (they are people after all), but the lack of distance between the actor and person they are performing reduces that novelty, so there is less engaging tension in reading them. A very non-human character can open up opportunities to act as something unusual and yet intuitively, even comfortably, familiar. R2-D2's shape is rather like a mailbox, a trash can, a lampshade, or perhaps a mid-century modern vacuum cleaner. The Star Wars stories give him functions that respond to those visual suggestions: this droid will indeed deliver messages and clean up messes. But he can also do things that *things* cannot; there are delightful moments in live-action Star Wars where the droid offers emotional support, for example. Part of R2's charm is his ontological duality as an appliance and a friend. So while his design and personality have elements of the familiar, the combination of those into one character is quite unusual (unless you consider preceding sci-fi robots, but even that is part of R2's familiarity; his divergences from *them* are novel). Similarly, Ewoks from *Episode VI: Return of the Jedi* are warriors who are also teddy bears. These are delightfully nonsensical surprises, and the juxtaposition within them (such as the Ewok's cuddly violence) heightens this duality of novel familiarity.

Puppetry artists often use the term "anthropomorphizing" to describe what it means to move and voice an object as if it were a person. This is analogous to what animators do in rendering talking animals, trees, and teapots with personalities. What makes such characters fun is our unspoken, shared assumption that only people can talk, and only people are intelligent. So the material character sits in a paradoxical place as an impossible being because it appears to communicate, feel, respond, and act independently. Because of this status, the material characters offer two initial surprises that emerge from the duality of novel familiarity. We are surprised when we first see them, the moment we first behold their bodies and shapes, because they are both adjacent to and outside our current experience (we might feel the same way encountering an especially strange fish). But that is just the first surprise, that they exist. The second surprise is that next, their actions or behaviors will do one of two things: they'll either satisfy or upend expectations that appearance sets. For example, when Chewbacca first appears in the original 1977 film, talking casually to Obi-Wan Kenobi at the cantina bar, he's as delightfully odd as every other creature in this zoological establishment. But when Obi-Wan introduces him to Luke as a "copilot," things change right away. The fact that he's highly intelligent upends expectations made on the basis of his appearance, which is something like a cross between a bear and a lion—neither of which operate complex machinery on Earth. So then, once we've gotten over that and absorbed this paradox into our understanding of his character, his human-like aptitude becomes simply a fun characteristic of this unique, now-familiar being.

Absent Presence

In material character performance, the human being—sometimes more than one human being—who animates the figure is often hidden yet felt. In live performances, a puppeteer might be visible or fully concealed, but their presence is always a part of the illusion's success, in some way peering through—literally or figuratively. Puppetry scholar Steve Tillis writes in "The Actor Occluded: Puppet Theatre and Action Theory" that there is a tension between the puppeteer/operator and character that "invariably exposes the presence of the operator … even as it occludes that presence by taking focus as the site of the operator's performance" which he connects to the "ontological paradox of the puppet" (Tillis 1996, 115). This phenomenon is part of what I call absent presence, a duality that carries significant meaning in live or recorded performance, and which can take many forms. In a theatre production, the performer working with a material character might be fully or partially visible, or they might work from a concealed location, even inside the character, or well off-stage. If the puppeteer is exposed, the audience is often implicitly asked to regard the material character as equally or more important than the performer animating them, or pretend that the human isn't there at all (puppeteers are often costumed in ways that assist in backgrounding their faces and bodies while foregrounding the puppet). Similarly, when an actor wears a mask, we are asked to replace our perception of their face (which we know is there, behind it) with this other image.

For realistic live-action material characters, such as those we see in Star Wars, the puppeteer/actor/performer is absent from view (most often hidden inside the character, or visually erased in post-production), but they are actively present as well. Using their voice, their actions, and their choices, they *present* themselves through their engagement with the material. Human beings, whether they are holding rods attached to the puppet or off camera operating a remote control for an animatronic movement, make choices as part of their craft in bringing their character to imagined life. The same is true for a suit character or a mask, which also rely on the performer's impulses and choices.

Puppetry artist Roman Paska suggests there is a "confrontation or interaction between performer and object" which is "the core of the art" of puppetry (Paska 2012, 139). I believe this extends to any material character, whether a puppet, suit, or mask—it engages with the actor in a way different than if they were performing another human being because of that confrontation, or the gentler term *collaboration*. In Star Wars, there is a dynamic energy in the creature, droid, or masked person that cannot exist without the relationship. In a 1980 interview with *Rolling Stone*'s Timothy White, Anthony Daniels said this about his collaboration with C-3PO, the suit: "between us, we make up a somewhat beautiful piece of sculpture." White notes in his article that "Daniels frequently discusses C-3PO in terms of 'we'" (White 1980). There is something of that "between" in what I'm calling the duality of absent presence that often constitutes the successful material character. Actor Peter Mayhew's eyes were Chewbacca's, peering through his furry visage (they are now the eyes of actor Joonas Suotamo, who understudied with Mayhew prior to his death in 2019). In practical material characters, we see the *work of* the actor or puppeteer/operator in the movement of the arm, the ear, the choice of a head-turn, and the energy between that creature and their scene partners who are breathing (or pretending to breathe) the very same air. Performance-capture CGI uses close-fitting suits and chroma key markers (dots on the actor's face) to "capture" the performer's motions to drive an animated image that is not them, presenting a virtual intermixing between flesh and image with its own absent presence. For example, the sequel's super-villain, Snoke, relies on Andy Serkis's unified body and voice in playing very nuanced human actions and minute human-like facial expressions that read in extreme closeup. Though design and performance collaborate to express distilled evil, Serkis's absent presence allows him to bring in more subtle expressive choices as well because of that unity between body and voice and the detail of facial tracking. There is a compelling tension in sensing something hidden, something *human*, with any type of material character.

Limited Limitlessness

Puppetry enthusiasts often celebrate the apparent limitlessness of the art form. As Tillis puts it, "puppets can be designed and manipulated to look and move more or less like *anything*" (Tillis 1996, 112). This broadening of possibility is due to the distance between the human character and material character—the latter can do things that the person cannot (like fly or be tiny), which can make them seem magical. But magical is not the same as boundless. Tangible stuff is restrained by natural laws. Limits in design and function can help determine characteristics and actions. Successful material characters enact their powers by asserting limitations and inventing within boundaries. The power dynamic popularly associated with the word "puppet"—when used as an insult to describe a person controlled by others—collapses here. Those who work with puppets do use the word "controllers" to reference gadgetry; but these figures are no more controllable than they are boundless. Many puppeteers will tell you: it's actually the puppet that's in charge because performing figures assert themselves in their limitations, as well as their affordances. In examining the theoretical writings of early 20th-century Russian puppetry artists Nina Simonovich-Efimova and Iulia Slonimskaia, Dassia Posner identifies a paradox she names "disobedient obedience" to describe their collaborative/listening approach to working with material objects, which ran counter to prevalent modernist ideas about a puppet's lack of agency (Posner 2014, 131). John Bell suggests that "the puppeteer is playing with a certain lack of control, and experimenting with the different possibilities of the puppet while constantly being aware of how the puppet's structure determines movement" (Bell 2013, 7). Artist Felice Amato writes that her experimentations with puppetry revealed a certain humanity through imperfection: " ... the patch of wool on the side of the face that doesn't fully match the rest? It agitates a bit, a quality so very human" (Amato 2016, 27).

On the desert sands of Tunisia in 1976, Star Wars' first droid prop/costumes (for *Episode IV: A New Hope*) caused a great deal of difficulty. They introduced all kinds of unexpected problems, and often didn't do what Lucas hoped or envisioned. But the hard limitations helped build successful characters. Some of C-3PO's movement vocabulary arose from mime-trained Anthony Daniel's negotiations with the stiff suit and all it could not do—the fact that he could not run led to the creation of his signature shuffle. Actor Kenny Baker discovered one of the few ways he could puppeteer R2-D2 well from the inside was to enact a rocking back and forth motion when the droid was upright—thus creating R2's signal of excitement or distress (Robb 2012, 54). The puppet's difficulty navigating wheels through sand made his adventure in Tatooine more grounded in the realities of his harsh environment. These two material characters came into being by working with and around limitations discovered through the human-material engagement.

Notwithstanding these successes, Lucasfilm turned to CGI as a wholesale problem-solver for the next trilogy, the prequels, allowing them to get around the limitations that frustrated them in the earlier films. Negative reactions to the CGI characters, voiced by unhappy fans and critics, illustrate the importance of understanding the duality of limited limitlessness. The Platt College of

San Diego, which specializes in Media Art, describes the prequel's CGI opportunities and failures this way:

> Understandably, as filmmakers and art directors were no longer limited by the physical world around them, they were free to create entire worlds digitally. This freed them from the laws of physics to the expensive and time-consuming process of building things by hand. However, the results weren't always positive, and this divorce from the physical world may be a key reason why the prequels weren't as loved as the original trilogy.
>
> *(Platt College, n.d.)*

Digital character distance is seductive: a creature or droid can be any shape and size because they are free from so many restraints imposed by practical material. But those missing restraints are actually a gift, a power the practical character brings to bear in engaging audiences not only in their plausibility and unity within a live-action world, but in terms of their relatability. Like the tangible R2 of *A New Hope*, we might also struggle to walk down a sandy desert slope; his difficulties endear him to us. The duality of limited limitlessness can serve the CGI animation, however, if the character is restrained by boundaries. For example, the tracking of an actor's face grounds a performance capture CGI character like Snoke. Creators can use their limitations to create character; the Kaminoan's glide is analogous to C-3PO's awkward gait; both take a limitation posed by their type of material and turn it into a character quality. As our intermediaries in this strange world, material characters—particularly tangible ones—create a meaningful connection with us through that negotiation. Puppeteer and filmmaker Ben Page suggests in his video essay *Beyond Baby Yoda* that "puppetry is the intangible made tangible. It is a direct link into the world of someone's imagination, their dream world that is simultaneously grounded in a real world where the physics of gravity, light and mass apply" (Page 2020). Those elements are boundaries, rules of Earth we all must obey. Good puppeteers often frame limits in terms of the figure's meaningful, essential role as an intermediary between us bounded humans and a potentially boundless world of the imagination.

Considering Star Wars' return to tangible effects in the trilogy sequel, Lev Grossman writes that "the most important, most un-simulatable quality of real objects is their raw physicality, a stubborn intractability and imperfection that's profoundly convincing" (Grossman 2017, 71). Here Grossman is describing objects in terms of personality traits, "intractability and imperfection," which echoes what puppetry artists share about a figure's agency to "shape and create," as Posner puts it, by refusing to comply with orders and, instead, inviting collaboration. This is their duality of limited limitlessness at play.

Living Death

I do not mean to suggest that material characters are zombies, but they do carry a paradox in their pretending to be sentient, breathing, living beings that continue to fascinate puppet theatre scholars. To Kenneth Gross, puppets can seem "fiercely alive, yet never quite living" (Gross 2014, xxiii). According to Dassia Posner, Penny Francis has ascribed the term "life-death" to "the idea that an object can be inanimate and yet simultaneously appear to contain life" (Posner 2014, 131). In considering the integration of puppets with people in theatre, performance scholar Ada Nutu writes: "As a lifeless object the puppet cannot truly experience emotional states but can only project them. The puppet can never truly live as much as the actor in performance can never truly be lifeless" (Nutu 2013, 203). But there is a lot of conversation among theatre scholars about whether a puppet is ever truly "inert." John Bell, who asserts that "the fundamental juxtaposition of living and dead provokes a continually charged situation" in puppetry (Bell 2013, 6), has pointed to how puppets and masks made of wood, hair, or other natural fibers might carry with them the memory of past life (Bell 2013, 220). African American object performance expert Paulette Richards is an animist who does not subscribe to the modern West's view of objects as inanimate, as lacking any spirit or life within them. Claudia Orenstein points out that indeed many people and cultures "do not articulate distinct dichotomies between animate and inanimate, living and dead, seeing all matter as endowed with spirit, or as providing sites for hosting a world of passing beings: divine, demonic, or the spirit of the deceased" (Orenstein 2014, 3). Dassia Posner analyzes how Slonimskaia "makes a distinction between dead and lifeless;" how "lifelessness infers that the puppet simply awaits animation" (Posner 2014, 137). This interpretation of the puppet—and by extension other types of material characters—means that the figure is inviting and meaningful in a state of vibrant stillness.

Star Wars material characters' living death duality is deployed as a story device that relies on the potential in stillness, the not-really-deadness of its droids in particular. In the second season of *The Mandalorian,* living death duality comes into play in a touching material character scene where a non-human creature partially animates a "dead" droid. In this second episode of season 2, we meet a suit character called the Frog Lady (this is her actual name, performed by Misty Rojas) who finds herself struggling to communicate urgently with Din Djarin. She grows frustrated by their language barrier, as they sit aboard his damaged ship, and they appear to be at a helpless impasse. Casting her large eyes about the cabin, the Frog Lady discovers an inanimate droid discarded in the corner, which the viewers of previous episodes might recognize as a humanoid droid named Zero. In their next scene, Din Djarin finds that Frog Lady has wired up a contraption to Zero, so that when she speaks into a microphone attached to him, his voice translates what she's saying into

English, as if he is himself speaking. Distance prevents this moment from being grotesque, but it's the living death duality that makes the scene so powerful in its strangeness and cleverness. In a way, Zero is brought back to life through this puppeteering by the Frog Lady, yet has no agency of his own. The very sense of what life is gets tickled in this all-material character scene.

In cases like this, a material character's living death radiates meaning in a number of ways simultaneously. Zero's crumpled and apparently inert body, clearly "dead," still signals in its material makeup that there was once activity here, a personality. It also suggests future activity—he's a machine, and can therefore be fixed. The duality of living death means a material character like Zero has a resonance and power when it's not moving—because unlike a corpse it is not dead; rather, it's waiting to be alive again through make-believe. We saw this before in the reanimation of the "dead" droid IG-11 in the first season of *The Mandalorian*. The material character is a real thing that requires pretending—requires fiction and play—to drive it. Theatre scholar Carolyn D. Roark calls the puppet "a corpse in reverse" because of its paradoxical lifelessness and "potential for momentary animation" (Roark 2009). Kenneth Gross has a similarly poetic take on this status: "A puppet in its very stillness and abandonment may be charged with potential motion, becoming an object of reverie, patiently awaiting some further life" (Gross 2011, 66).

Real–Fiction

Practical material characters and some digital puppets can, and often do, actually exist. In the fictional performance, and in the real world, that paradox brings material characters an added dimension. On set, a material character's tangibility can invite interactive physical impulses in their human castmates: Chewbacca might pull Leia into a spontaneous hug, C-3PO will bang his metal hand on R2's domed head in anger, and Poe Dameron can greet his beloved BB-8 by scratching his metal sides like a dog. These interactions are not only playful, they support the pretense that these non-humans are really there, really alive. Yet we know they are fictional, of course, because Wookiees don't exist. Actors and audience both behold Chewbacca with the knowledge that he's made up, and yet there he is, real as a carpet.

In the actual world, some Star Wars material characters resume their lives as pretend beings who both exist and don't. R2-D2 isn't real, and yet there are R2s all over the world you can touch and talk to (I've met several). These are often animatronic puppets operated by remote control where makers and cosplayers gather. Droid builder and VFX artist Jessica "Psy" DeLacy is one of many makers who build these true-to-life droid puppets and then animate them (via remote control) at a variety of events. Some of these droids are even cast in Star Wars films, where they play themselves. The same is true for stormtroopers performed by the 501st Legion, a charity that organizes events where participants dress as highly authentic-looking Star Wars characters (most famously, groups of stormtroopers who often push wheelchairs in children's hospitals or appear in parades). If you attend such an event, you can hang out with these Star Wars material characters as yourself, without any acting, because you are in the real world, not a play. Material characters are make-believe, yes, because C-3PO isn't really a robot (there is an actor inside pretending); Boba can't fly and doesn't really live in outer space. Yet, there they are. The screen or stage is replaced by the framework of the parade, the club event, the convention, or the amusement park. The material character packs themselves wherever they go.

Real–fiction duality also gives material characters the power of interdependence. They invite play because they need someone to make them move—to touch, remotely operate, or inhabit them. The material character is in this way incomplete, a part of something else. Gross places the puppet in a "family of things partial, fragmented, and broken, a family of relics, remnants, and skeletons" (Gross 2011, 95). A material character is partial and fragmented because of its need to collaborate (a mask is only part of a face of a character). It can be broken and relic-like because it is a piece of life somehow remaining when life (performance) is taken away. This is one way that real-fiction duality makes the material character uniquely engaging: what is broken asks to be fixed, what is skeletal asks to be identified, what is partial begs to be made whole. These are invitations—to fill in the story, to ask questions, to seek solutions to puzzles.

FIGURE 2.2 R2-D2 out for a stroll among regular folks

Just as the archeological aspects of the Star Wars thing aesthetic entice fans and writers to fill in story gaps, character backgrounds, and side plots, the things themselves invite actual real-world making. Curious engineers and "maker" hobbyists see the legless spherical droid BB-8 on screen and wonder not just "how did they make that?" but "how can I make it?" The real–fiction duality of material characters inspires theatrical playfulness and invention.

This invitation can be embedded within a material character's original creation. Lev Grossman's conversations with *The Force Awakens* creature effects supervisor, Neal Scanlan, reveal an approach to building a fictional character, via carefully chosen and integrated materials, which lend it a certain real-ness that begs to be animated:

> "Each one is a little piece of theater," he says, "and I think that's what the viewer picks up on." He builds them out of foam latex and high-end aeronautical carbon fiber, silicones and urethanes. Chewbacca's skin—in case you ever wondered about it—is hand-knitted, as in with needles, and then each hair (it's a mix of yak hair and mohair) is knotted to it individually. As a result it moves with the physical heft of a real organic creature's pelt. In a very real sense the creatures become performers just as much as the actors are.
>
> *(Grossman 2015)*

The movement of that cleverly woven yak hair (which holds the novel familiarity of a real animal) connects Scanlan, the craftsperson, to Chewbacca, and makes that artificial being appear more plausible through his thoughtful choices in design and construction. The theatre he speaks of here, as I see it, refers to that art form's bringing together of concepts, materials, and people to make something that is pretend, yet utterly real at the same time. Material characters hold this duality in their makeup and in their performance, so it reflects that idea of theatre back into whatever they do, wherever they go—whether it's to the stage, the set for a recorded performance, a parade, or even a children's hospital.

The five dualities of material characters—novel familiarity, absent presence, limited limitlessness, living death, and real-fiction—together offer a toolbox for creators, performers, and audience members to tell compelling stories in collaboration with stuff. Material characters might bring a number of these dualities into their performance, enabled by distance, and in some cases made brighter by the power of distillation.

Conclusion

I offer the terms *distance, distillation,* and *duality* to parse out and explain, in a clear and accessible way, what material characters offer. *Distance* is the literal and figurative gap between the material character and the human. *Distillation* is the material character's special ability to perform concentrated ideas. *Duality* is their power to be at least two things at once, often paradoxes offering narrative opportunities both within and beyond the fiction. I organize these terms into an alliterative trio to make material character powers more memorable and simpler to explain. I use film creatures and droids as illustrative examples, but the "Three D's" apply to material characters in any performance format: theatre and other live settings as well as film and television. Star Wars has offered a way to explain the Three D's, and these terms have, in turn, helped me discover the depth of material character contributions to meaningful storytelling in this popular culture epic. The following chapters investigate those discoveries in detail.

References

Amato, Felice. 2016. "A Split Broom for Legs: An Amateur Looks at the Puppet as Material Allegory." *Puppetry International*, Spring and Summer, (39): 26–8.

Arnold, Gary. 1977. "'Star Wars' (PG)." *The Washington Post*, May 25, 1977. https://www.washingtonpost.com/wp-srv/style/longterm/movies/review97/starwarsarnold.htm.

Bass, Eric. 2014. "Visual Dramaturgy: Some Thoughts for Puppet Theatre-Makers." In *The Routledge Companion to Puppetry and Material Performance*, edited by Dassia N. Posner, John Bell, Claudia Orenstein, 54–60. New York, NY: Routledge.

Bell, John. 2013. *American Puppet Modernism: Essays on the Material World in Performance*. New York, NY: Palgrave Macmillan.

Blumenthal, Eileen. 2005. *Puppetry: A World History*. New York, NY: Harry N. Abrams.

Brooker, Will. 2020. *Star Wars*. London, UK: Bloomsbury Academic.

Francis, Penny. 2012. *Puppetry: A Reader in Theatre Practice*. New York, NY: Bloomsbury Academic.

Gross, Kenneth. 2011. *Puppet: An Essay on Uncanny Life*. Chicago, IL: University of Chicago Press.

Gross, Kenneth. 2014. "Foreword." In *The Routledge Companion to Puppetry and Material Performance*, edited by Dassia N. Posner, John Bell, Claudia Orenstein, xxiii–xxiv. New York, NY: Routledge.

Grossman, Lev. 2015. "A New Hope: How J.J. Abrams Brought Back Star Wars Using Puppets, Greebles and Yak Hair." *TIME Magazine*, December 14, 2015, 56–75.

Jones, Basil. 2014. "Puppetry, Authorship, and the Ur-Narrative." In *The Routledge Companion to Puppetry and Material Performance*, edited by Dassia N. Posner, John Bell, Claudia Orenstein, 61–68. New York, NY: Routledge.

Nelson, Victoria. 2003. *The Secret Life of Puppets*. Cambridge, MA: Harvard University Press.

Nutu, Ada. 2013. "Alterity and Puppets in Contemporary Performance." *Theatrical Colloquia (Colocvii teatrale)*, no. 15, 200–216. Central and Eastern European Online Library.

Orenstein, Claudia. 2014. "Introduction: A Puppet Moment." In *The Routledge Companion to Puppetry and Material Performance*, edited by Dassia N. Posner, John Bell, Claudia Orenstein, 2–4. New York, New York: Routledge.

Page, Ben, director. 2020. *Beyond Baby Yoda—The World of Puppets.* YouTube. https://www.youtube.com/watch?v=YDAO6KGaqcc.

Paska, Roman. 2012. "Notes on Puppet Primitives and the Future of an Illusion." In *Puppetry: A Reader in Theatre Practice*, 136–140. New York, NY: Bloomsbury Academic.

Platt College. n.d. "Star Wars | Visual Effects through the years." Platt College San Diego. Accessed November 5, 2022. https://platt.edu/blog/a-breakdown-of-the-visual-effects-used-in-the-star-wars-franchise/#0.

Posner, Dassia N. 2014. "Life-Death and Disobedient Obedience: Russian Modernist Redefinitions of the Puppet." In *The Routledge Companion to Puppetry and Material Performance*, edited by Dassia N. Posner, Claudia Orenstein, John Bell, 130–143. New York, NY: Routledge.

Posner, Dassia N. 2014. "Part III: Contemporary Investigations and Hybridizations." In *The Routledge Companion to Puppetry and Material Performance*, edited by Claudia Orenstein, John Bell, Dassia N. Posner, 225–8. New York, NY: Routledge.

Roark, Carolyn D. 2009. *Research at the Ransom Center: Death and the Puppet*, blog post. Harry Ransom Center, Ransom Edition (Spring 2009).

Robb, Brian J. 2012. *A Brief Guide to Star Wars: The Unauthorized Inside Story of George Lucas's Epic.* Philadelphia, PA: Robinson.

Salisbury, Mark. 2018. *Moviemaking Magic of Star Wars: Creatures & Aliens.* New York, NY: Harry N. Abrams.

Sunstein, Cass R. 2016. *The World According to Star Wars.* New York, NY: William Morrow Publishers.

Tillis, Steve. 1996. "The Actor Occluded: Puppet Theatre and Acting Theory." *Theatre Topics*, 6 (2): 109–119.

White, Timothy. 1980. "'Star Wars': Slaves to the 'Empire.'" *Rolling Stone*, July 24, 1980. https://www.rollingstone.com/culture/culture-news/star-wars-slaves-to-the-empire-61931/.

Williams, Margaret. 2007. "Including the Audience: The Idea of 'the Puppet' and the Real Spectator." *Australasian Drama Studies*, (51): 119–132. International Index to Performing Arts.

WIRED. 2022. "Every Stormtrooper in Star Wars Explained by Lucasfilm." YouTube. https://www.youtube.com/watch?v=m4LFX-RWfn4&list=PLh4sGfPOCWCuvh-QkhZ7O8YPFl3dw_OGJ4&index=29.

PREFACE TO CHAPTERS 3 & 4

One of the most memorable moments in cinematic history is Darth Vader's line to Luke Skywalker, "I am your father" in *Episode V: The Empire Strikes Back*. For audiences who saw it for the first time in the theaters in 1980, this was many revelations rolled into one. This scene is preceded by Luke's training with another thoughtful revealed material character named Yoda. The mask (Vader) and the puppet (Yoda) were at the center of the original trilogy and played large parts in both deepening and strengthening a story that was to become iconic in Western popular culture. The revelation in both cases was part of a confrontation between human hero and material character (Luke was the human in both cases for *Empire*), a pattern repeated in the prequels, sequels, and in the inaugural streaming TV series, *The Mandalorian*, decades later. Each of the three cinematographic compositions features a hero transformed by their relationship with a puppet or a mask—sometimes both.

Chapter 3 brings closer focus on the first meeting between Luke and Yoda in Episode V: *The Empire Strikes Back* in order to illuminate the depth and potency of puppet–person relationships, particularly in this film. It then pursues a comparison with a newer puppet that captured the global imagination: Baby Yoda from *The Mandalorian*. Chapter 4 analyzes the trajectory of Darth Vader's mask in all three film trilogies, following its incarnation through revelations and the expansion of the mask in Kylo Ren. Returning to my schematization, these analyses demonstrate how distance, distillation, and duality of puppet and mask support depth in story and theme.

DOI: 10.4324/9781003137559-4

3

POWERFUL, PUPPETRY IS

How Two Yodas Make Meaning

The First Yoda

Reflecting on the original trilogy, film critic Roger Ebert called *The Empire Strikes Back* "the best of three Star Wars films, and the most thought-provoking," and "one of the most visionary and inventive of all films." Ebert attributes this in part to how the movie "surrenders more completely to the underlying mystery of the story. It is because of the emotions stirred in 'Empire' that the entire series takes on a mythic quality that resonates back to the first and ahead to the third. This is the heart" (Ebert 1997). A small green puppet named Yoda played a critical role in lending *Empire* its depth in both emotion and the story's meaning. He may have become a CGI digital character later, but it is the success of the original puppet in *Empire* that made the character so iconic and impactful. In this first section, I offer context surrounding Yoda's creation, then take a close look at how the puppet is used in his scenes with Luke in *Empire*, before outlining how distance, distillation, and the dualities of this material character ignite transformation in the saga's hero.

A New Kind of Muppet?

In the 1970s, when Lucas was working on the first two Star Wars films, puppetry was established in American public consciousness by popular variety-show television and children's educational programs. Puppeteer Fred (Mr.) Rogers delivered his consequential speech about educational television funding to the United States Congress in 1969, just months before the premiere of *Sesame Street*. *The Muppet Show*—a prime-time variety show for adults, but also beloved by kids—was particularly popular during the late 1970s and early 1980s, when the first Star Wars trilogy was being made. As puppets were popularly aligned

DOI: 10.4324/9781003137559-5

with children's education and comedy entertainment in the United States, it is understandable that Lucas had mixed feelings about casting one as Yoda, his first emotionally complex non-human character. It's clear watching the film what the character needed to be, which was something not introduced before in Star Wars: a realistic-looking creature who speaks English, interacts with humans fluidly, and expresses a range of subtle and nuanced emotions. He could not be silly, like the Muppets. In his book *American Puppet Modernism*, John Bell writes about how Lucas's Star Wars approach was in some ways following a path laid by twentieth-century American puppeteers like Remo Bufano, who understood puppets' talent for managing the metaphysical and metaphorical realms such as those that Luke encounters. Bell points out how Lucas nevertheless feared the high-stakes choice to use a puppet, and cites this statement Lucas made in an interview years later: "if that puppet had not worked, the whole film would have been down the tubes … if it had been [Jim Henson's Muppet] Kermit running around in the movie, the whole movie would have collapsed under the weight of it" (Bell 2013, 157). As it turned out, the Muppets creator himself, Jim Henson, was wrestling with nearly the same challenge at that time. Henson and his team were working on realizing the vision for *The Dark Crystal,* a film that would take a wildly different approach to puppetry (ultimately released between *Empire* and *Return of the Jedi*). Referencing Caseen Gaines's book, *The Dark Crystal: The Ultimate Visual History,* James Whitbrook describes Henson's challenge this way for the technology and design website, Gizmodo:

> Jim Henson was eager to craft a world of puppets that looked unlike any of his work on the then-rising success of *The Muppets*. It wasn't just tone or genre that Henson wanted to distance himself from, but the physicality of the beings themselves: He didn't want puppets that, like Kermit, were obviously made from felt and ping-pong balls. He wanted his fantasy project to star characters that felt real and as if they lived as part of an actual world.
>
> *(Whitbrook 2019)*

Lucas's team had a similar desire for this new Star Wars puppet: to avoid the Muppets' presentational, recognizably handmade and artificial look. Yoda would need to be unlike Kermit the Frog, even though he was also designed to be green, diminutive, and swamp-dwelling, because Kermit looks like a felt puppet, not a frog. Whatever Yoda is (and his species was kept elusive) he would need to look like that kind of creature, and not comment on it. Lucas's and Henson's teams ultimately arranged to share personnel and expertise in problem-solving for Yoda, which is how puppeteers Frank Oz, Cathay Mullen, and other Henson Company artists came to work on the new Star Wars film (Whitbrook 2019).

According to J.W. Rinzler's *The Making of The Empire Strikes Back*, filming Yoda's scenes on the Dagobah set was laborious and difficult (Rinzler 2010, 226). The slow, repetitive practice recorded in Rinzler's daily descriptions of the Dagobah shoot are similar to what one might expect in live theatre rehearsals, particularly where puppets are involved. The final results in the film show how well the puppeteers brought this character to life by finding just the right rhythm and tone to his novel syntax (both created and voiced by Oz), marrying it with his gestures, coordinating with eyes and ears, and punctuating certain actions. This expert, attentive puppeteering paid off in successful performance and influenced the direction of both Henson and Lucas: "everything Oz and the rest of the team Henson had lent to the film were lessons learned to help bring the Gelflings, Skesis, Podlings, and rest of Thra's denizens to life in the enchantingly realistic way that would eventually earn *The Dark Crystal* its place in cinematic history" (Whitbrook 2019). For Lucas's next film, *Episode VI: Return of the Jedi*, he would bring even more realistic, *Dark Crystal*-like beings on board, like the drooling Jabba the Hutt and his fierce Rancor creature.

A Puppet Teacher

Yoda deepens the trilogy's themes and ideas, chiefly by teaching Luke Skywalker what "the force" really means. The saga's hero begins to transform into a more mature, less self-involved person through his engagement with this puppet. Yoda's appearance is preceded by a number of other material character performances that support the deeper territory this material being would enter into with Luke. *Empire* begins on the ice planet Hoth, where Luke faces an attack by a Wampa while riding on the back of a Tauntaun. Next, he faces down several enormous Imperial Walkers. Luke's warrior status is established vis-à-vis these battles against creatures and objects, but they are all external obstacles. Yoda is the first material character to emotionally challenge Luke, and he guides the hero's growth in a more internal direction. On Dagobah, Luke's person-ness stands out for the first time in Star Wars. Mark Hamill drily reflected later, "I was the only human on the call sheets for months" (Becker and Burns, 2004). This misty planet appears to have no lights, no cities, and no people. Luke had already assured his mechanical companion, R2-D2, that the place is safe for droids, but it quickly becomes clear, upon landing, that it's not. As they disembark, a swamp creature swallows R2, then vomits him onto the shore. Dagobah—Luke's Jedi training ground—is a place that literally spits out technology.

To fully appreciate the puppet-human relationship between Yoda and Luke, it's important to review what happens in their first four scenes together—so I will here offer a summary. Their first encounter takes place shortly after Luke and R2 land on the boggy planet and begin to set up camp. Luke is talking to

FIGURE 3.1 Yoda hosts Luke in his hut in *The Empire Strikes Back* (LUCASFILM)

the droid about a funny feeling he's having when a voice startles them from behind. Luke whirls around, pointing his blaster at what is revealed to be a small, gnome-like creature who exclaims "away put your weapon, I mean you no harm" (Kershner 1980). Luke slowly complies, but almost immediately dismisses the creature's offer to help him. Luke tells the stranger, "I'm looking for someone," and he replies, "found someone you have," but Luke shakes his head, saying that he's actually there to find a "great warrior." The creature responds with one of his many now-iconic lines: "wars not make one great." He then begins rummaging through Luke's camp, laughing and tossing supplies around as he searches messily for something he wants. He nabs Luke's flashlight, then whacks R2 with his cane when the droid tries to retrieve it, shouting "mine!" Luke responds to this pest with exasperation, until the creature reveals that he knows Yoda—and convinces a skeptical Luke to follow him.

Their next scene together shows them in a small hovel, where the creature is serving stew. R2 peers through a window to see the stranger fussing at Luke to relax and chat as they shelter from the rain. But Luke is eager to see Yoda, and loses his patience with the delay. After a minor tantrum, in which Luke tosses down his host's meal in frustration, the creature begins to address the air above him, saying "I cannot teach him. The boy has no patience." A discorporate voice replies, which Luke soon recognizes as his late mentor, Obi-Wan Kenobi. Realizing his mistake, Luke rushes to explain himself, bumping his head on the ceiling as he tries to stand up and appeal to his teacher. That this green creature is Jedi Master Yoda is a surprise character revelation for Luke (as it was for the 1980 audience). It is also a reversal: now the hero is the fool, and the pest is the sage. Commander Luke Skywalker, destroyer of the Death Star, has failed miserably at the first test. He not only learns at this moment how poorly he has behaved in the past (he's apparently been observed by Yoda his whole life), he's behaving badly—and rather childishly proving the very point being made about his impatience—right now, even after the realization.

By their third scene, Luke has begun his Jedi training; we see him running and leaping through a grueling course among the vines and trees while Yoda (as a puppet, able to ride on his back) spills truths about the force into his ear. As they break for the day, Yoda sits still on the misty forest floor and Luke notices something—a feeling coming from a cave. At his teacher's urging, Luke descends into the dark, foreboding place among lizards and snakes, where he soon encounters a dream-like vision of Darth Vader. They draw lightsabers and fight. Luke swings and decapitates the phantom enemy, his helmet-mask rolling onto the ground. The mask explodes and reveals an image of Luke's own face inside it, replacing Vader's. The scene cuts to Luke gazing at his own visage. Outside the cave, Yoda sits quietly in the bog and grunts knowingly.

The fourth Yoda-Luke scene is similarly one of the most iconic and meaningful moments for the saga's struggling hero. Luke's ship has begun to sink further into Degobah's swamp, which distracts him from his training—it is his only way off this planet. Though Luke had just that moment been practicing moving objects with his mind (rather puppeteer-like), he immediately rejects Yoda's suggestion that he use the force to lift the giant X-wing out of the water. He argues that moving a ship is entirely different from lifting stones off the forest floor. Yoda objects: "No! No different! Only different in your mind. You must unlearn what you have learned." Luke gives it a try, but fails—the ship moves for a moment, but then sinks deeper into the swamp. Exhausted by the effort, Luke turns to Yoda, protesting that it's just too big, that he cannot lift it. Yoda replies "Size matters not. Look at me. Judge me by my size, do you?" Luke responds with a head shake, but he had indeed judged him by his size and is still, now, inhibited by his beliefs about objects and his relationship with things around him.

Throughout these early training events together, Yoda takes moments of Luke's frustration as teaching opportunities, revealing the deeper nature of this fictional idea of the force. He describes it as a binding energy that flows around them, telling Luke that he should feel it not only between himself and other living beings, but between himself and objects like the ship. The screenplay calls for the teacher to guide his pupil into a new way of imagining the world about him, to "unlearn" his inherited assumptions, such as the relationship between size and strength.

Yoda and Luke's transformative interactions depend on all three powers of material character performance: distance, distillation, and duality. Yoda's distance from humans opens the door for him to be very small and even a bit animal-like in a way that is not sub-human, but rather potentially beyond or above Luke and his kind. As an ambiguous species, his gnomish appearance helps Yoda to trick Luke, to take advantage of the young hero's narrow view of what his mentor is supposed to look like. When Luke first meets the creature, he is barely interested, and does not for a moment consider he's found the Jedi master he's come looking for. Once Luke reveals his blindness, and his narrow-minded assumptions, Yoda begins to rummage through his things and make a scene, to play the part of a pesky gnome. In retrospect, it seems he was testing Luke, or even initiating the first lesson—which he himself embodies as something (some*one*) rather opposite of what the naive hero envisioned. The contrast between Yoda's stature in the story and his physical size hint at the potential for expanding our regard for non-humans. Yoda's size is also interesting in his environment: he fits in on Dagobah, but his home shrinks the hero, making Luke look ridiculous with his head bent and bumping against the ceiling.

In his body and movement, Yoda is the distilled version of an old man and the many rich signals that caricature can hold. The long, deep furrows across Yoda's brow suggest years devoted to contemplation. Yoda's design expresses many other exaggerated indications of age as well: baldness, skin blemishes (his complexion is almost the color of rot), stooped and shrunken posture, hardened nails (claws, in his case)—all reinforced by the dialog and performance, which altogether contrast Luke's youthful naivete. Yoda materially embodies the fallacy of Luke's wrong-headed assumptions, such as what a Jedi master is supposed to look like, and the idea that physical prowess is a primary source of power. Interestingly, even after Yoda reveals himself to Luke for what he is, the creature remains stubborn and quirky—his performance as a pesky old man wasn't all pretend. The puppeteers' artistry helps stretch these characteristics in different interpretive directions, and Luke is forced to see Yoda—and soon, everything else around himself—in a different light. Those wrinkles are not signs of decaying old age, but the earned marks of a sage, his furrows carved by years of deep thinking. Yoda the puppet is an ideal teacher for Luke because he is corporeally representing and communicating to Luke how wrongheaded he is.

Yoda's dualities also deepen the meaning of these critical *Empire* scenes. Makeup artist Stuart Freeborn sculpted the image of a human being into Yoda's face by referencing his own (Rinzler 2010, 94). This resulted in a novel shape of Yoda's green visage combined with the familiar arrangement of a human being's eyes, nose, and cheeks. The duality of novel familiarity also comes through in the interaction between Luke and Yoda: Mark Hamill's unforced, relaxed earnestness with Yoda, combined with a little humor, echoed other puppet/person relationships on television at the time. Yoda's choices and in-the-moment responses to Hamill echo the easygoing, lively exchanges between puppets and people on *Sesame Street* and *The Muppet Show*, which were normalizing relationships between furry and fleshy beings in the 1970s and 80s. And therein also lay another familiar element to Frank Oz's voice and performance style. Oz was performing many of the world's most famous Muppets at the time, including Miss Piggy, and *Sesame Street's* Grover and Bert. In 1980, Yoda would need to counter the energy of a Muppet in the audience's minds, yet there were helpful bits of these characters in Yoda's personality: Grover's goofiness and Miss Piggy's fierceness are both there. In fact, Miss Piggy (quite a celebrity at the time) made a surprise visit to the Dagobah set; Rinzler's descriptions of this prank (Rinzler 2010, 225) highlight how successfully Yoda uses his comic predecessors' qualities to create a multidimensional new character—for in the film, Yoda is both deadly serious and, at times, quite funny. The duality of Yoda's novel familiarity to a 1980s Muppet-influenced audience may have also encouraged people to accept this figure, while expanding prevailing notions of how a puppet is to look and perform. Yoda's absent presence duality also is potent in this way; there's a literal Oz behind the curtain (or in this case, beneath the floor) who collaborates with the puppet, its gadgetry, and other puppeteers as he voices the character's lively exchanges. Oz's vocal and movement choices, as well as his inventive approach to characterization, all conspired to make Yoda appear not only viably real and alive, but compellingly human, as if he carried within himself a piece of the invisible people—the puppeteers beneath him—who bring him to life.

The duality of real-fiction also makes Yoda the perfect vehicle to instruct Luke at this critical juncture in the trilogy's story. Yoda brings to the film a deeper understanding of this abstract notion of the force—to Luke and to the audience. Yoda's very existence asks us to believe in what's not real. Of course, this is true for many fantastical elements of the space saga, but this complex, articulate puppet adds another layer of make-believe. When Luke fails to lift his ship from the water, Yoda lectures him about the meaning of the force—how it puts objects, creatures, and things on a more even plane as energetic, interconnected actants. His real puppet claw pinches Luke's fleshy shoulder as he tells him "luminous beings are we, not this crude matter." Luke misses the whole message, though, responding despondently with "you want the impossible" as he walks away. Yoda then proves what is possible by lifting the ship slowly out of the water with a concentrated effort of his mind and gesture, raising it up with his tiny claw and guiding it safely to shore before Luke's incredulous gaze. Of course, Yoda is himself impossible, so who better a messenger? Yoda's puppet-ness, the fact that he himself is an object, embodies what he is trying to teach Luke about the force: it's not about the power to manipulate objects, it's about our relationship to them. He asks Luke to feel the energy "between you... me... the tree... the rock..." That is, in fact, one of the best ways to describe the art of puppeteering.

Baby Yoda

Yoda has been lasting and influential, but there is no greater proof of his power than his wildly popular semi-reincarnation in the early 2020s. Four decades after *Empire*, the first live-action Star Wars streaming series, *The Mandalorian* (2019–), revealed a tiny green puppet both similar to and almost the opposite of Yoda. The material nature of both the masked Din Djarin (Pedro Pascal) and the puppeteered Baby Yoda (revealed as "Grogu" in Season 2) are at the heart of what makes the story work. At this writing, the saga of Grogu continues in anticipation of more live-action appearances, but there is a story arc to the first two seasons of *The Mandalorian* that captures how well the puppet generates meaning, from the first episode of the first season, to the finale of the second. I will here summarize key elements of that story and then look at how the powers of distance, distillation, and duality make Grogu's performance so compelling and consequential.

FIGURE 3.2 Baby Yoda (Grogu) becomes a beloved companion to the masked Din Djarin in *The Mandalorian* (LUCASFILM)

Mask Meets Puppet

Concept-designed by Christian Alzmann, Grogu was built and performed by Legacy Effects as a child-aged creature of Yoda's species. He was first known popularly as Baby Yoda (though he is not Yoda) and is referred to in the first season as The Child. He is a puppet (technically, he's several puppets) requiring multiple Legacy puppeteers working together to animate his face and body. He is much smaller than Yoda and puppeteered with a combination of rods at his limbs and remote-control animatronics.

The first episode of *The Mandalorian* sets up the viewer in the world of *Episode VI: Return of the Jedi* (1983) with a particular emphasis on the practical creatures, droids, and masks featured in the original trilogy. The masked, nameless "Mando" (short for Mandalorian) is introduced as a professional bounty hunter who works alone. While not exactly a villain, neither does he project a heroic persona; he is here to do a job and speaks very little. In the first episode, he takes commission from the bounty hunter guild leader, Greef Karga (Carl Weathers), to capture a particularly valuable and elusive "asset." Once Mando (revealed later to be named Din Djarin) reaches the location of the asset, he finds it extremely well-guarded. He and his competitor, the bounty hunter droid IG-11 (voiced by Taika Waititi), team up to fight their way through. Once they succeed, the two use a "tracking fob" to find the asset, which leads them to an egg-shaped floating container not much bigger than a bread box. The droid and masked man approach the container and look down at it together as it opens. The camera's perspective shifts to the egg's and shows two expressionless metallic faces gazing downward. Then we shift to their perspective. Inside the container is a small blanket. A green paw reaches up, then pulls the blanket down to reveal a green face with long pointy ears and two enormous, blinking black eyes. It makes a cooing sound. Mando is surprised to see a child—he says the creature is reportedly 50 years old. IG-11 explains that not all species age at the same rate, and draws his weapon to kill it. Before the droid can shoot, Mando blasts him in the head and IG-11 falls lifeless to the ground (distance, of course, allowing for this act of violence on a material character to be not-gruesome). In a gesture that suggests Michelangelo's *Creation of Adam* in silhouette, Mando reaches his gloved finger toward the figure, and a wee claw emerges to touch it. The episode ends there, with two material characters shrouded in mystery, making a tentative and very human connection.

This is a significant moment because Mando is the modern archetype of a jaded male antihero who shuts himself off from others and tries to exhibit no feelings. His decision to save the child's life, and his impulse to reach out to touch it, are early signs that there may be a crack in that metaphoric (and for the material character, literal) armor. In a future episode, he will commit fully to the mission of rescuing the creature from hunters like himself. And by the end of the second season, he will have succeeded at returning The Child to "his kind" (the Jedi) and proven himself a changed man. So, this is the arc to the two-season story: Mando (revealed to be named Din Djarin) grows from a frozen man into a caring father. Grogu softens him, exposes him, and awakens his humanity. In Chapter 4, we will look at the ways a Star Wars helmet-mask character can move between human and material character status by donning and removing the mask, in a way that usually represents good versus evil. In the case of *The Mandalorian*, the unmasking is personal and happens as the direct result of the masked man's relationship with the puppet.

The Child's Powers

Grogu (aka The Child) does not directly teach Din Djarin the way that Yoda teaches Luke. It is their proximity and developing relationship that impacts the man over time. Din Djarin's battle with a material character called the Mudhorn exemplifies particularly well how the learning takes place, often in non-verbal action. In this season 1, episode 2 scene, Din Djarin has agreed to retrieve a Mudhorn egg for the Jawas in exchange for his stolen ship parts, and goes to the creature's cave. He prepares to enter by cocking all of his weapons. His armor is full of things like flamethrowers, and he has recently disclosed to his companion, Kuiil, that weapons are his religion. But they do little to help him here: when he disturbs the Mudhorn, this dinosaur-sized animal throws him up into the air out of the cave and into the mud, ruining his armor. The Mudhorn then charges Mando like a bull, tossing him to and fro like a ragdoll. The man's considerable fighting skills and tools, which have served him well until this point, prove useless. He is able to protect The Child slightly—by moving his cradle out of the way—but not himself. Finally, dizzy and beaten, Mando gets up on his knees and feebly points his dagger forward in the direction of the Mudhorn who is coming at him in a final, fatal charge. But then the scene cuts to a closeup of a tiny green claw rising up in a gesture reminiscent of Yoda's. The puppet's face squints as if in concentration, its ears draw down, and the Mudhorn is lifted slowly and helplessly up in the air, suspended as if by The Child's magic. The giant beast falls to the ground and dies, leaving the dazed Mandalorian to stab it with his teensy dagger, as if to finish her off himself. So, Din Djarin survives not because of the soulless objects of war he worships, but thanks to a little organic being with invisible, mysterious powers. The outcome of Din Djarin's Mudhorn battle echoes Luke's confrontations with dangerous material characters and over-reliance (and faith in) technical might in *Empire*. Depending on machines—and trying to behave like a machine himself as a masked character (Kornhaber 2019)—is a flaw Din Djarin must overcome. He will have to make an inward shift to start believing in the intangible (in his case, love).

Grogu's distance, distillation, and duality support his ability to affect Din Djarin's transformation. Grogu's distance from the human is most starkly applied to scale. He is very, very small compared with all other creatures in the story, especially humans. Though he is very different from a human infant, he is human-infant-sized, which makes him appear vulnerable. He is often carried and passed from person-to-person like a baby. It is also more surprising and meaningful, as it was with Yoda, to see such a tiny being move such large bodies with the force, like the enormous Mudhorn. Grogu's distance enables distillation in his appearance: because Grogu could be a baby without being a person, designers had the liberty to create enormous eyes and wide, flexible ears that make him even more essentially childlike. Grogu's irresistible cuteness is partially attributable to a human being's own natural responses to these kinds of proportions. *Bustle* entertainment writer Shannon Carlin offers this scientific explanation:

> His infant-like features—That large round head! Those big eyes!—are the scientific definition of cuteness, according to Joshua Klapow, PhD, a clinical psychologist. "Any features that remind us of infants or babies will draw us in," Klapow told Bustle back in November. "It is our natural parental instincts to protect or at least feel connected to babies."
>
> *(Carlin 2019)*

Grogu's exaggerated features support his allegorical presentation—he is curiosity, dependence, and impulsivity embodied. In the way Yoda is a distilled representation of extreme age, Grogu is all youth. Grogu is not an individual child so much as every child: he is actually named "The Child" for the entire first season. He is the essence of (any kind of) sentient, intelligent creature in infancy. And this distillation is held at a distance from us human viewers: because he is a material character, we see his infant self more clearly, outside of our personal experience with children, but also *because of* our personal experiences with the nurturing impulse. The feelings Grogu evoked as a beloved and popular character in the early 2020s are due at least in large part, as Carlin suggests, to our shared instinct to protect the young.

The duality of Grogu's novel familiarity is also part of his charm and effectiveness. Again, he reminds us of babies and puppies, but he also reminds us of Yoda. The puppet's design echoes Yoda in appearance, yet surprises us with the differences between the characters, which we must anticipate and guess before and as they unfold. Grogu is known to audiences—he looks a lot like a visit from our old friend—and yet he's never been seen before. He is something beloved and familiar, recombined and made new.

A Material Character Goodbye

The way the little guy unmasks this lone bounty hunter, again, constitutes the story arc of the first two seasons of *The Mandalorian*. Their emotional parting in the season 2 finale demonstrates their mutual affection at its most moving, and shows material character meaning-making at its Star Wars best. In the final moments of the episode, Din Djarin and his companions have just been rescued by Luke Skywalker, now a Jedi master. Luke is there to take Grogu away so that he can be trained as a Jedi, and Grogu is clearly reluctant to leave Din Djarin. The man picks him up to say goodbye, and Grogu reaches forward to touch the mask. Din Djarin removes his helmet (an act strictly forbidden by his Mandalorian code), revealing a face that is trying to contain his emotion. Grogu strokes the man's cheek.

The closeup moment of the Grogu-Din Djarin goodbye exemplifies how compelling this moment-to-moment communication can make a pivotal emotional scene between two material characters. Adam Chitwood describes it this way for the entertainment website, Collider:

> it's right here, in this moment, that The Mandalorian pulls off its biggest surprise—it hits you right in the heart. The Mandalorian, who so steadfastly has refused to remove his helmet for two seasons, did so in Season 2's penultimate episode in order to find Grogu. And now he removes his helmet to say goodbye.... Not in a time crunch, not to get to the next level of the plot, but to show Grogu—his child, for all intents and purposes—his full self. He lets his guard down, his hard exterior, to comfort Grogu and assure him everything is going to be alright. OOOOOF. Right. In. The. Feels.
>
> *(Chitwood 2020)*

One of the reasons this is such a powerful moment is that we do not actually know why Grogu is stroking the mask (before Din Djarin removes it)—he does not speak and there are no subtitles to translate his coos, so we the audience (just like the fictional characters in the story) have to engage really deeply to interpret—we are more than just receivers, we are readers. And because we cannot be certain, there are multiple possibilities. Grogu might be asking permission indeed, or he might be asking Din Djarin to show his face so that he can touch it. Or he might be stroking the mask because he thinks that's his face. The puppet's gesture communicates deep, distilled emotion, yet leaves space for the onlooker to engage in interpretation. All of this is part of the art of the material character, and speaks to its powers.

Eventually, Din Djarin puts Grogu down, but the creature clings to his leg, like a toddler, as Luke waits patiently by the door. They are at an impasse. Then there is a familiar, mechanical beeping sound. R2-D2 (not seen at all in the series up to this point) pulls in from behind Luke and reveals himself to Grogu. The little puppet releases Din Djarin and begins to approach the droid. R2 brings his "feet" under him, then tips forward so that he's able to meet Grogu's gaze. No human, not Grogu's own father figure, nor even the mighty Luke Skywalker himself, can convince Grogu to leave. It appears only another puppet can do that. As Grogu joins R2, Luke and Din Djarin look over their heads at one another—these two heroes transformed by little green puppets—and nod.

Though the power of this scene lay in the mask-puppet relationship, that puppet-puppet connection merits a closer look as well. Grogu's moment with R2-D2 is all the more compelling for their contrast in size. R2, always one of the shortest of Star War characters, adjusts his body to look down—to gaze directly at an even smaller one.

Grogu bears resemblance in distilled qualities to the droid, which is part of what makes their scene together so fitting. R2 and Grogu's similarities are not at all visual (in fact, the two are opposites in this respect—one hard and mechanical, the other soft and organic) but they embody similar ideas, and both had a profound impact on audiences when first introduced to the world. Popular response to Baby Yoda was similar to the droid's introduction to the world decades earlier. *Smithsonian Magazine*'s Clive Thompson writes:

> With its stubby little body, blooping voice and wide round eye, R2-D2 was a curiously endearing machine. Fans went crazy for the droid, knitting winter hats in its shape and building computer cases that looked like its body. Even *Star Wars* actors went a bit googly-eyed when they were on the set alongside the droid. "There is something about R2-D2," as the robot's original designer, Tony Dyson, has said, "that people just want to cuddle."
>
> *(Thompson 2014)*

Both Grogu and R2 are over 50 years old in *The Mandalorian*, yet kid-like in their designed and performed precociousness—they both project the essence of the child. And like R2, Grogu's language is distilled. He communicates in the vernacular of non-verbal puppets, with abstract sounds and gestures. He is even more distilled in voice and movement than Yoda in this way—for everything he wants to say has to be conveyed with a gaze, a move of the ears, a head turn, a point, a groan. Much of this movement language is universally understood because the gestures many humans use are common signals of distress, surprise, and joy. It was a powerful choice to make the final moments of this finale a wordless conversation between two material characters: Grogu and R2 were saying things to one another, perhaps, that are not for we human grownups to hear. Like the fictional people in the room, we in the audience must watch closely to try to interpret the combination of beeps and looks.

Conclusion

Puppets Yoda and Grogu are teachers in what they do, and what they represent. Both sit at the heart of a Star Wars story, wielding powers of distance, distillation, and duality in their relationships with the central protagonist's journey. Yoda trains Luke in the ways of the force by embodying its tenets.

Grogu transforms Din Djarin by inviting the frozen man to care for him as a vulnerable child. Both enacted the duality of novel familiarity on audiences familiar with popular culture figures and extended the art of film puppetry through their successful design, performance, use, and contextualization in their stories. Though there are many other puppets in Star Wars, these two deserve particular recognition for demonstrating a material character's potential to bring depth and meaning to a pop culture epic.

References

Becker, Edith, and Kevin Burns, directors. 2004. *Empire of Dreams: The Story of the 'Star Wars' Trilogy.* https://subslikescript.com/movie/Empire_of_Dreams_The_Story_of_the_Star_Wars_Trilogy-416716.

Bell, John. 2013. *American Puppet Modernism: Essays on the Material World in Performance.* New York, NY: Palgrave Macmillan.

Carlin, Shannon. 2019. "Baby Yoda Was the Most Googled Baby of 2019 & It's a Mood." *Bustle.* https://www.bustle.com/p/baby-yoda-was-the-most-googled-baby-of-2019-its-a-mood-19443446.

Chitwood, Adam. 2020. "The Mandalorian Season 2 Finale Explained: Why It Nailed the Ending." Collider. https://collider.com/the-mandalorian-season-2-finale-ending-explained/.

Ebert, Roger. 1997. "The Empire Strikes Back Movie Review (1997)." *Roger Ebert*, April 1, 1997. https://www.rogerebert.com/reviews/the-empire-strikes-back-1997-1.

Kornhaber, Spencer. 2019. "'The Mandalorian' Season Finale Scrambles Man and Machine." *The Atlantic*, December 30, 2019. https://www.theatlantic.com/entertainment/archive/2019/12/mandalorian-season-finale-scrambles-man-and-machine/604237/.

Kershner, Irvin, director. 1980. *Star Wars: Episode V—The Empire Strikes Back.* Screenplay by Leigh Brackett and Lawrence Kasdan. Lucasfilm Ltd.

Rinzler, J. W. 2010. *The Making of Star Wars: The Empire Strikes Back.* New York, NY: Random House Worlds.

Thompson, Clive. 2014. "Why Do We Love R2-D2 and Not C-3PO?" *Smithsonian Magazine*, May 14, 2014. https://www.smithsonianmag.com/arts-culture/why-do-we-love-r2-d2-and-not-c-3po-180951176/.

Whitbrook, James. 2019. "Star Wars Empire Strikes Back & Dark Crystal History Connection." Gizmodo. https://gizmodo.com/how-the-empire-strikes-back-helped-shape-the-look-of-th-1837516288.

4

I FIND YOUR LACK OF FACE DISTURBING

The Mask Performance of Darth Vader (and Friends)

Taken together and viewed in hindsight, the story of both George Lucas's trilogies is the story of Darth Vader's mask: how it came off (originals), and how it got on in the first place (prequels). Both trilogies lead up to the mask revelation. Vader transforms from material to human character at the end of *Episode VI: Return of the Jedi*, and then we see the reverse at the close of *Episode III: The Revenge of the Sith*. Decades after the prequels, a new generation of Star Wars creators working for Disney would make Vader appear again, in the form of a disembodied, burned Vader mask, to inspire a new masked villain, Kylo Ren (Adam Driver). This chapter explores the revelation of Darth Vader's character in the original trilogies and prequels (1977–2005) and compares it with his successor, Kylo Ren of the sequel trilogy (2015–2019). Together, they demonstrate a range of profound ways distance, distillation, and duality can play out with the mask material character.

Darth Vader was first revealed in 1977, four and a half minutes into the first *Star Wars* film. He brought the duality of novel familiarity at first glance. Vader was a thing both alien and recognizable. His helmet-mask (was it a mask, or his actual head?) echoes the samurai, but Vader was entirely new. He appeared humanoid, but it wasn't clear whether he belonged to our species or to another. This ambiguous presentation made Vader one of Star Wars' most intriguing puzzles. As a material character, Vader crosses more categories than others. He is both a helmet-mask and a suit character because his entire appearance is inorganic: there is not even an inch of exposed skin; he looks crafted all of a piece. Vader emits a mysteriously mechanical breathing sound, and his chest is made of colorful buttons suggesting he is at least partly a machine. Because of the mask, he has no facial features to indicate his personhood, though he speaks and stands like a human somehow altered. He is not as mechanical as the droids; like the stormtroopers he moves fluidly—and like them, is clearly a bad guy. He is of

DOI: 10.4324/9781003137559-6

FIGURE 4.1 The mask and costume of Darth Vader (LUCASFILM)

unknown origin, which is true for Luke and others, but it is particularly tanta-lizing because Vader's very species has never been seen before. In his 2016 book, *The World According to Star Wars,* Cass R. Sunstein declares that Darth Vader has no rival in Star Wars for his lasting appeal (Sunstein 2016, 78). He points to nov-elist Lydia Millet's 2002 essay *Becoming Darth Vader,* which analyzes the implica-tions of that mask in the context of what Vader means to her symbolically as a figure who embodies, among other things, a cool distance from others. Here is what Millet writes about the mask and its relationship to Vader:

> To state the obvious about Vader, he was a faceless man behind a ferocious black mask, protected by his anonymity .... We might imagine behind the mask the face of Hitler, the face of a monster, the face of a machine, a skull with gaping eye sockets, or far, far more, something horrifying and primeval, beyond words as well as beyond sight, unspeakable. There was no end to what we could imagine, and for that reason the mask was, needless to say, far more compelling than anything that could ever be behind it, as is the way with masks.
>
> *(Millet 2002, 133–4)*

Millet is spot-on regarding the mask: its allure as a thing of concealment and mystery invites us to imagine, and Vader is particularly evocative in his use of it.

Without all of these characteristics of the mask Millet describes here, and what the story does with it, there would have been less depth to Star Wars. So it was particularly smart of Lucas's creative team to draw out that question—What's behind the mask?—and keep him a material character until the very end of the original trilogy, *Episode VI: Return of the Jedi*, in 1983. Lucas saved the ultimate revelation of Vader for the climax of the trilogy itself. So audiences got six years of Vader as a helmet-mask character, and a few minutes of him as a human named Anakin. Perhaps part of the critical failure of Lucas's prequels was that a human character, Anakin, could never compete with the mask.

But in the meantime, hints to answer the question were dribbled out like breadcrumbs in *Episode V: The Empire Strikes Back* (1980) and *Episode VI: Return of the Jedi* (1983) using the tools of material performance. The most powerful example is when audiences in 1980 got a clue during a scene between an Imperial officer and Darth Vader about a third of the way through *Empire*. Entering his boss's chambers for a word, the Admiral stands at attention, to wait for him. His face reacts slightly as if discomforted by whatever he's gazing at. The view cuts to reveal it to us: through the teeth-like cracks of a metal contraption, we see Vader's scarred bald head just before the helmet-mask is placed upon it with a mechanical sucking noise. It is a major revelation, and yet the greatest function of the mask, to hide the face, remains in force because we are only shown the back of the head. Filmed and edited as an accidental glimpse into something private, this tease leads to further questions and deeper involvement, and positions us as voyeurs who get a piece of the puzzle we weren't supposed to have. Is this mask meant to conceal his ugliness, keep him alive, or both? Is he strong without it, or broken underneath it? Where did this mask come from?

But most importantly, this wordless moment of material performance in 1980 revealed the mask as something *removable*, with a flesh-and-blood being beneath, suggesting Vader was once something other than what he is now. This is where distance comes into play: here was a character able to separate from a human performer. Vader's mask, as it turns out, is not the same as the character, but a thing apart from him. And he has a relationship with it. This has many implications, but the most meaningful for the *Episode V: The Empire Strikes Back* plot are that this detachable mask may have been placed on a human Vader, and that the mask is transferable. These two offerings come together in the *Empire*'s much-analyzed Dagobah cave scene, where Luke confronts a phantom version of Vader. When the mask part of Vader's helmet explodes, revealing Luke's own face inside it, it's an object warning Luke that he could himself become Vader—or that perhaps he already is (as is often the way with good visual symbols, there are myriad layers of meaning). This moment relies on the separation of the material helmet-mask enabled by its distance; it holds the power to depart from its wearer and find another host. This moment of wordless material performance is, of course, key to the mythical father-son confrontation that later serves as the climax of *Empire* when Luke (and, in 1980, the world) learns simultaneously the truth about Vader and about Luke's father with the single line: "I am your father" (Kershner 1980). For

Luke, part of the horror of this revelation is that it changes his very understanding of his place in the world. Luke's admiration for his late father, coupled with his hatred for Vader, is what has fueled his desire to become a Jedi. Vader is also a distilled representation of evil for the audience—his ruthlessness is both intimate (he routinely chokes people to death with his thoughts when they displease him) and political (he is an agent of genocide and tyranny). Luke's late father was known to him as a heroic Jedi killed by Vader; he is the antithesis to Vader in the story's lore up to this point. Now, with one short sentence, Luke's beloved father and most hated enemy fuse into the same person. The up-is-down reorienting that Yoda's training demanded is now fully coming into force. Two material characters, a puppet and a mask, collaborate in this bookended way to transform the central hero.

The final film in the original trilogy reconciles this father-son tension in a way entirely dependent on the mask. By the start of *Episode VI: Return of the Jedi* (1983), the question of what's behind that mask has been answered in terms of identity but has yet to be answered visually. Neither Luke nor the audience has actually seen Vader's face in those six years. That mystery can only be satisfied with an image, and that image arrives in the film's final scenes. It is an incremental reveal that takes place at the story's climactic confrontation between Luke and his father. After a protracted and dramatic lightsaber fight, one that is both psychological and physical, Luke finally bests Vader. But rather than kill him, as the emperor commands him to, Luke looks down at his own mechanical hand, covered in a black glove that resembles Vader's. His gaze suggests a dawning fear: that his actions are indeed, literally, turning him into his father—transforming him from a man with a material hand to a whole material character. Luke discards his weapon and tells the emperor he is willing to die rather than submit to that. In response, the emperor begins to electrocute Luke as the injured Vader slowly picks himself up to stand beside his master and watch. The editing shows Vader's helmet-mask gaze shifting between the emperor and Luke, who cries in agony and begs his father to help. After thirty agonizing seconds, Vader suddenly lifts the emperor and tosses him into the belly of the ship. Mark Clark describes the scene this way in his book, *Star Wars FAQ*:

> Vader's internal battle to turn away from the Dark Side, and his ultimate decision to destroy the emperor, unfolds entirely without dialogue. More impressively still, it's told without a human face for the pivotal character; audiences only see Vader's blank, robotic mask. His swirling emotions are conveyed entirely through body language, deft editing, and John Williams' tense, haunted musical cues (featuring a ghostly-sounding choir). It's visual storytelling of the highest order.
>
> *(Clark 2015, 217–18)*

The fixedness of this mask makes Vader simply unreadable, drawing out the tension and forcing the viewer to rely on the simplified language of its shifts in gaze. We only see the reflection of blue lightning from Luke's torment reflected in Vader's shiny mask as he watches his son suffer nearly to death. There are no eyes or moving brows to show us a window into Vader's inward psychology, which stands in great contrast to Luke's transparent, even extreme facial expressions throughout this scene.

In the next scene between them, Luke carries his injured father—this large, limping villain—in an attempt to escape with both their lives as the Empire's space station crumbles around them. Stopping for a breath, the injured Vader asks Luke to remove his mask so that he can look at his son with his own eyes. Luke hesitates, knowing that this will kill his father, but Vader/Anakin tells him that there is nothing to prevent that, so Luke complies. As he gently removes the mask, Luke and the audience see a chalky, wounded, vulnerable old man—remarkably soft and human. In this scene, we see a transition from material to human character performance. Until this point, Darth Vader *is* the mask, so the metamorphosis is as literal as it is symbolic. Distance allows this separation: Vader and Anakin split with its removal. The materiality also plays upon its ability to express extreme, distilled ideas because the mask has been immobile and concealing, and once peeled away allows for the fuller expression of nuance and change. In the scenes prior, the critical interactions leading up to their confrontation, Vader had already begun to push against the purity of his villainy, growing slightly more nuanced. In an earlier scene, where Luke has surrendered to Vader and they await a conveyor to the emperor, Vader calls Luke "son" and gingerly admires the lightsaber he crafted before ascending the elevator with him to the emperor's chambers. Luke tells Vader he "senses" his affection, and he repeats this again later, even as they fight viciously with their sabers. Vader finally acts on that conflicted feeling by saving Luke's life. When he does that, he is already less Vader—for Vader is a thing of no nuance. So now, the mask must also come off literally, just as the mask performance has begun to fall away figuratively. Luke had set out to "turn" his father at the beginning of the film, but what he ends up doing is inspiring his father to separate himself from Vader. At the moment of unmasking, they become two distinct beings—one human and the other material. The shock of the revelation of that soft human face, after six years of concealment, was all the more powerful for the mask's distillation of hard, uncompromising evil. We soon learn that Luke was able to convey his father's body back to Endor, where his rebel friends await, and where he stands alone to burn him on a funeral pyre—mask and all. Soon after, Anakin appears as a force-ghost in the robes of a Jedi, joining the smiling tableau of family and friends at the triumphant end to the original Star Wars trilogy. The duality of Vader-Anakin is resolved in the appearance of Anakin's recovered humanity, freed from the material prison of the Vader mask-costume left behind to burn. Vader and Anakin are now corporeally separated, fully distanced in two places: one is an inanimate villain made of material (which is in turn being converted to smoke), the other an ephemeral spirit.

Mask Revelation in the Prequels

The prequels are a mirror to the original trilogy in many ways, rewinding into the past to explain its greatest mystery: how the masked Vader came to be. Audiences witnessed in *Return of the Jedi* how Anakin won back his humanity, and in doing so regained his face. The prequels explain how he lost his humanity and got the mask. Both feature the mask in pivotal scenes (trilogy climaxes) of Anakin-Vader's transformation and take full advantage of its powers as a material character.

Anakin's fall to the Dark Side amounts to a distillation of his evil impulses in this story, represented by his transformation into the masked, material Vader. In the prequels, Anakin transitions in stages from a kind-but-conflicted young man into a distilled, resolved villain. What happened behind the Vader mask in the original movies is played out by human character acting in the prequels—actor Hayden Christensen performing Anakin in a way that is fully exposed and passionate. In the story of the prequels, that passion is part of his downfall. By the second film, Anakin is an adolescent who shows the first sign of murderous capacity by hunting down the Tusken Raiders who killed his mother, and massacring their entire clan, including the children. His willingness to betray and kill grows more concentrated in the waning minutes of the final installment, *Episode III: Revenge of the Sith*, leading up to his masking at the end of the film. That final hardening of Anakin's soul transpires when he finally loses the epic duel with his beloved mentor, Obi-Wan Kenobi (Ewan McGregor). The film then portrays the physical transformation of Anakin, the person, into Vader, with droids operating on his scarred, dismembered body, placing metal prosthetics onto his burned limbs as he cries out in agony. The editing shifts to a camera angle revealing Anakin's point-of-view, and the mask appears to come onto our face. In a move that resembles the closing of a coffin, this shiny, iconic mask then fills the screen in gigantic profile as it hinges to gradually cover that face and land in its familiar, formidable shape (an impressive cinematic experience if you saw it on a giant theater screen for the first time in 2005). Covered and disappeared, Anakin rises at the end of this scene, as a complete material character.

Many things are taking place simultaneously in this scene, all enabled by distance, distillation, and duality. The characters that impose that procedure—the emperor looking on, the mechanical surgeons—are creating a material character by fusing the human with the non-human. That distance emerging between the two is tight, and it will add to the ever-present tension that characterizes Darth Vader. The expressive human, Anakin, is encased in the mask to become a rigid, distilled embodiment of evil. The duality of novel familiarity is present in the recognition of the iconic twentieth-century mask of Vader himself, made new by this visual revelation of his practical genesis. And there is a powerful contrast being drawn between the character with humanity (the human Anakin with a movable face), and the character who has lost it (the material, Vader). The transfiguration both symbolizes that contrast and enacts an ontological change. As a material character, a new story of selfhood emerges for Anakin/Vader: he has the duality of being, at least figuratively, both alive and dead. Anakin is dying, but the machine revives him. It allows him to live, but it also kills what Anakin was, what he lived for. This scene was much analyzed at the time for its expansion of the mythic father-son relationship. In the 2007 History Channel documentary, *Star Wars: The Legacy Revealed,* humanities scholar Camille Paglia compares Darth Vader to Hamlet's armed, ghostly father, while others align him with Lucifer because of his fall to temptation and thirst for power. Mary Henderson refers to his transformation into a machine as a personalized hell for such a passionate young man (Burns 2007). In becoming the helmet-mask character, Anakin loses his human attractiveness, his ability to touch, kiss, and even make eye contact, all at once. This echoes the climax of the original trilogy, when the aged Anakin asks Luke to remove the mask so that he can see his son with his own human eyes.

Eileen Blumenthal writes that puppets can carry their "performance history" and "outward appearance" forward in time in a way that humans cannot (Blumenthal 2005, 198). The extreme novel familiarity in Vader's mask would render it just as potent in the 2010s' sequel trilogy as it had for those last few minutes of the prequels. Even without a performer inside, Vader's mask makes a statement; in the sequel films, he becomes a super-vibrant object.

Return of the Mask in the Sequel Trilogy

The sequel trilogy is about how scavenger Rey (Daisy Ridley) and ex-stormtrooper Finn (John Boyega), along with their friends, fight the tyranny of a second empire called The New Order. Their nemesis is a masked villain named Kylo Ren (Adam Driver) who, like Vader, is the tool of a somewhat distant, menacing ruler named Snoke (Andy Serkis). Kylo Ren enters *Episode VII: The Force Awakens* a mysterious masked man; it's gradually revealed he is/was Ben Solo—son of Han and Leia—turned to the Dark Side of the force by Snoke. There is a new hero for the villain to hunt: Rey, who (like Luke before her) eventually develops empathy for her enemy in the course of the trilogy story. In *Episode VIII: The Last Jedi,* she tries to convince Kylo to "turn" from the Dark Side. Kylo is eventually redeemed; he turns back into Ben with Rey's help in the climax of *Episode IX: The Rise of Skywalker.* Though Kylo Ren hasn't reached the pop culture stature of the original Vader (will anyone, ever?), he is nevertheless a very successful, surprisingly complex material character. What characterizes Kylo's journey are two things: his relationship to the distilled mask of the original villain, Darth Vader, and the way the story's creators use the new mask's distance to transition Kylo into and out of material character status.

Let's look first at this relationship between mask and mask, revealed in a scene between the two in the first sequel film. About an hour in, the masked

Kylo Ren is shown sitting alone, talking to some unseen presence. A spirit? Kylo seems to be praying to something because he is asking for forgiveness. He addresses the space as "grandfather" and asks to be shown "again" the Dark Side power to help him resist the temptations towards goodness. He promises to "finish what you started" (Abrams 2015). When Kylo stands up to leave, the frame reveals that he has been talking not to an ephemeral spirit or god, but to a material thing: the deformed mask of the late Darth Vader, which fills the screen, face-to-face with the audience through the camera. Yet it's not the iconic mask we know so well—not the hard, shiny, perfectly symmetrical head of that imposing villain. His iconic triangular mouth guard is split into shards like the broken teeth of a decaying corpse. The burned mask is messy and disfigured, a thing almost as uneasy to look at as the pained and injured face it once covered. Because of its distance from the human, Vader—now reduced to a plastic skull—has a very different performance than an actual skull or decaying human face. It reminds us of these things, and yet it is not these things, so it operates in the realm of simile; this is the duality of novel familiarity at work with the mask's distillation. The violence acted upon the mask in cremation (made palatable by distance—we see the mask burn, not Anakin's fleshy face) has made Vader's face compelling but not repulsively horrifying. This scene in *Episode VII: The Force Awakens* between the two masks (one inhabited by a living creature, one separated from its inhabitant) exemplifies how a material character, or a part of one, can separate because of distance and grow into something else, something both connected to and independent from its human performer. In this case, the mask has become a super-vibrant object, a non-sentient thing that is not quite a character in the story's treatment, but so much more than a prop.

Vader's distillation as a symbol of pure wickedness is now made literal. He has been melted down to his essence and made into a performing object that is soulless, a "twisted and evil" thing, as Obi-Wan once described him. It all echoes how Vader's mask came to be a burned, disfigured thing in the story (his face literally twisted now). The mask was last seen in 1983's *Return of the Jedi*. Near the end of the film, Luke burns Vader on a pyre in his mask and suit, his gaze turning upward along with the camera to follow the smoke— material transitioned as it floats up into the air towards the stars above. So the reappearance of Vader's burned mask in the Disney sequels (2015–2019) makes the husk of Vader a still-powerful presence, for it has lived even in its apparent inertness. Vader as a persona, a representation of evil, fascism—and its very irrepressibility—seems to resist even death and cremation. The material Vader is now even more distilled and more distanced from any human actor or character. Removed from the wearer, and distilled down to its essence, the mask is now even more Vader than Vader ever was. This is because it is not just Anakin who is freed from Vader, but Vader who is freed of Anakin.

As a living character, Vader was already a figure whose living death dual-ity had made him particularly formidable and ambiguous. Now, in *The Force Awakens* he is long since *very much dead*—the Vader mask and the identity it represented has been removed from the human body, burned up, his loud breathing silenced. Yet, given its interaction with Kylo Ren in this scene, the mask still has the power to act upon others as a distanced, separated thing. By Kylo's request, "show me again," we learn that he has reason, for clearly there is a precedent, to believe that Vader still has power to judge him, or to help him. He even begins the speech to Vader by apologizing to the mask for his own failures. Perhaps this is one mask communicating to another how to manipulate the human souls, the Anakin Skywalker and Ben Solo, that inhabit them—which speaks to a potentially spiritual aspect of a mask. Given all of this, it makes good narrative sense that Kylo's journey is one of failure to fill his grandfather's shoes to become the next Darth Vader. Star Wars is concerned less with literal death than the demise and resurrection of character ethos—and these material characters are critical to the redemption stories.

As we examined in *Episode V: The Empire Strikes Back* (1980), the discovery that Vader's mask could separate itself from his human occupant, as a distanced object, deepens the story at the heart of that first trilogy. In the later sequel trilogy, the mask's integrity as a removable thing is taken even further with Kylo Ren. The way in which Kylo relates to the mask both on and off of his face is part of his gradual uncovering and his evolution as a character. *Episode VII: The Force Awakens* (2015) introduces its helmet-mask villain bit by bit. It begins with his Vader-like, cape-flowing entrance early in the film flanked by an entourage of stormtroopers. But the differences soon mount. First and foremost, he does not keep his mask on as long as Vader once did, when he was the villain of the original trilogy. Kylo's face gets revealed well before the climax of the first film, and in a fairly casual manner. He is interrogating an imprisoned Rey, who resists, insulting her enemy as a "creature in a mask." He responds by simply pausing for a moment, and then removing the mask, before continuing on with his questioning. Rey's reaction reveals surprise, and adjustment: the face behind the mask is a healthy young person like herself. Locked in the eye contact this exposure allows, Rey not only resists Kylo's attempt to extract more information from her mind but reads Kylo's mind right back. She calls out his deepest fear, which is, of course, related directly to that mask, that he'll never measure up to Vader. Kylo's transparent, startled reaction (the first visible emotion seen in Kylo thus far) confirms her insight. And it is the first of what will be many examples of Kylo's inability to hide his feelings while exposed.

As casual as it may have seemed at first, this revelation is very significant in developing the new villain's character. We learn in that moment that the man behind the mask is not only young and healthy, in contrast to the scarred cyborg inhabiting Vader's helmet, but that his selfhood and physical survival are entirely free from this thing on his face. It reveals that Kylo merely wears the mask like a costume and disguise; it's optional. Distance enables this nascent villain to perform Kylo Ren while concealing his former and inner self, Ben Solo. Kylo's failure in this performance is the spine of the antagonist's trajectory in this trilogy story.

The sequel films make full use of Kylo's un-Vader-like freedom to don and remove the mask at will. This hopping into and out of material performance introduces a different type of dramatic tension for the new installment while building on what Lucas's trilogies introduced with Vader's mask. In the sequels, this back-and-forth switching communicates both the cause and flavor of Kylo's inadequacy. He is unable to fulfill the promise of the masked villain because he fails to perform Vader's legendary focused, distilled resolve. Pop culture writer Amy Richau suggests that Kylo wears the mask performatively, as a costume to make him look scary and to hide his wavering emotions (Richau 2018). But Kylo's Vader imitation is weak even with the mask because it lacks the requisite aplomb of the real thing, that outer wall, that reliable single-minded focus that characterized his idol. Kylo aims at distillation, at eliminating the parts of him that are human and nuanced, and selecting out only the hatred and malevolence—but he's not good at it. And that's not for lack of trying: Kylo works hard to prove his Vaderesque strength through cold acts of violence. The problem for him is that he can't seem to distill it—the material character eludes him. The internal conflict Vader exhibited only at the end of the original trilogy, in *Return of the Jedi*, is forefronted in Kylo from the beginning, and it's why this human character's collaboration with this mask is so meaningfully unstable. So while Kylo Ren is a material character, and must be in order to manage the duality of Ben Solo's performance, it is also a failed performance in part because the distillation can't hold.

Kylo the man is tormented—again, Hamlet-like—by the dread of having to do what he feels he must: kill his father, Han Solo. The mask plays a critical part in the inevitable father-son confrontation near the end of *Episode VII: The Force Awakens*. It is a highly emotional scene between an estranged father and son that recalls Vader and Luke's mythic confrontation and reconciliation in the original trilogy. It begins when Solo tracks Kylo Ren across a thin bridge inside the New Order's Starkiller base. He calls out to him by his given name, Ben. Kylo turns and they meet. Almost immediately, Han asks his son to take off his mask. Ben/Kylo complies, dropping it to the floor and facing his father—his flushed, emotion-ridden face fully exposed and set in eye contact. At the end of this scene, Kylo finds resolve and spears his father with his lightsaber. Before falling to his death, Solo reaches up and touches his son's face. It is a powerful moment for many reasons, but it is made richer by the absence of that mask. Kylo proves he is evil enough to kill his father while looking him in the eye (again, an echo of the maskless moment between father and son in the original trilogy).

In the sequel, *Episode VIII: The Last Jedi*, Kylo is nowhere to be seen in the dramatic New Order space battle that takes up the first ten minutes of the film. He does not appear until nearly every other major character has already shown up—it's as if his status update is saved for later. His mask is back on and it fills the screen. He seems to be on an elevator of some sort, on his way to see Supreme Leader Snoke (a CGI performance-capture humanoid). In a way, Snoke is the opposite of a Kylo—here is a material character who projects exactly as he wishes to: his booming voice and imposing, graceful body are both nuanced and unified while also performing a distilled embodiment of malevolence as he crinkles his misshapen face. Snoke begins the interview by inquiring about his apprentice's wounds. Kylo, kneeling and gazing at the floor, responds through the mask that modifies his voice, concealing his feelings both visually and aurally. Kylo dismisses his injuries as "nothing." Snoke responds by reprimanding him for his failure to live up to his family's evil legacy as a second Vader. Looking down at the upturned mask, which looks like Vader's from behind, Snoke interrupts the young man's excuses with an intimately whispered, emasculating command: "Take that ridiculous thing off" (Johnson 2017). Kylo slowly removes the helmet-mask to reveal his

FIGURE 4.2 Kylo Ren silently regards his mask in *The Last Jedi* (LUCASFILM)

scarred face, with tired circles under his eyes. Snoke describes what he sees now in the exposed face: that he has his father's heart in him (presumably a feeling of empathy), but Kylo almost shouts that he killed his father, without hesitation. Snoke raises his own voice and counters that the murder split him in two. This recalls Kylo's own admission to Han Solo that he was being "torn apart" by his feelings. And, with tragic irony, this moment confirms that the sacrifice was fruitless—even patricide did not fix the problem and make Kylo the resolved, unconflicted villain he's expected to become. Snoke scolds Kylo for his failures, then issues a final insult before he's dismissed: "alas, you're no Vader. You're just a child. In a mask."

In this scene, placed in this middle act of the trilogy, Kylo is not only failing to play the part, he's failing to conceal his failure. The mask is not doing the job he expected it to. Critic Julia Alexander analyzes Kylo as a man struggling with his own vulnerability, who "can't temper his emotions or control his facial expressions," suggesting that he wears the mask in part to conceal that problem, especially around Snoke (Alexander 2017). A moment later in the film, there is a wordless performance of the material character that amounts to a kind of climax for the mask, at least for this film. Kylo, alone after Snoke's dressing down, is shown in the exact same position as he was at the top of the scene, facing almost straight-on with the camera, filling the screen—only this time it's his naked face, not the mask's. He looks down and we see he's holding it in his right hand, facing upward; he's looking at it—almost as if the two parts of him are making eye contact. We have one more glance at his face, then suddenly Kylo takes the mask and bashes it hard against the wall of the elevator. In a fit of violence, he smashes the mask over and over, breaking both the glass of the room and the thing itself, leaving it commingled in a pile of violated, disorganized material on the floor. The final shot in that scene is a closeup of the broken helmet, recalling the image in the last film of Vader's destroyed mask. In this way, the character resolves the tension of this duality violently, by force. He can do this because the mask is distanced: it's something he can separate from himself, and something that can withstand a type of violence he himself could not. Having failed at performing the mask, Kylo destroys it.

It is particularly interesting to see the human character and the material character at the same time, in the same shot, gazing at one another. Here we have a character who is not only figuratively divided but is *literally* in two places at once: two ontological presences enabled by the separation which distance offers the mask. The man's two personas—Ben Solo (person) and Kylo Ren (a thing representing an idea)—are fighting one another. This wordless scene presents a visual metaphor of a person split in two.

Kylo's destruction of the mask makes him thereafter, at least for the duration of this middle film in the trilogy, an unmasked villain. Film critic Nick

Evans makes this point about Kylo's rejection of the mask: "Near the end [of *The Last Jedi*], he seems more resolved, especially after there is no longer a mask to hide the conflict in the man beneath it. By removing that mask, Rian Johnson may have given us the most complex Star Wars villain yet" (Evans 2017). Yet the building blocks of that evolution still rely on the power of that original material performance: distance allows for its on–off function and makes possible the distillation he attempts to reach in matching the outward design of the mask with inward actions. Distance enables Kylo to be both a masked and unmasked character who could separate from, and attempt to destroy, a part of himself.

There is a bit of play with the duality of limited limitlessness here as well. The way Kylo Ren's relationship to the mask is written, he is not dependent on it for survival, so the character could go in any direction with it—but at the same time, wearing it limits the actor's ability to perform with his face. Evans praised this decision to dispense with the mask so that Adam Driver's acting could contribute more range and express more nuance and change in the evolving, psychologically complex villain. This is true to the character type: the helmet-mask figure can make this transition. But it's the fact of that mask and the limits it places on expression that create that relief, that comparison, that need to remove. The duality of being both limitless and limited is part of the mask's special tension.

In the final sequel film, *Episode IX: The Rise of Skywalker*, Kylo Ren puts the mask back on in a way that reveals, even celebrates, his inward conflict for others to see. The mask is repaired by a mysterious group of primate-like material characters to sport red fissures at the crack lines, which was intended to outwardly express Kylo's inward fractured-ness (Lyne 2019). Kylo rejoins the Knights of Ren, a mysterious masked gang whose larger presence in this film hints at an origin story for the mask: it is not only a tribute to his grandfather and a transformational tool, it is an affiliation. The young villain fits in visually for the first time in this sequel trilogy with a group of warriors. Like the stormtroopers, clones, and Mandalorians, these knights seem to be defined by their masks. In re-committing himself to this group, and standing beside them, the masked Kylo Ren has an agenda and allegiance independent of his Darth Vader obsession. The mask is now part of his Ren-ness, giving him a belonging that is not tied up in bloodlines. It adds further tension to his struggle with dual identity, with his vacillating between allegiances both in his political actions and in his personal feelings, particularly towards Rey. The added complexity here is that no use of the mask is effective this time for Kylo/ Ben; it really is just a costume for the character, fixed or not. In his redemption scene with Rey, where she looks into the face of her now-maskless comrade, she calls him "Ben." The mask has no part in this scene, but the memory of it brings more significance to the exposed face in this very human moment at the end of Kylo's life.

Conclusion

These two villain journeys, told over the course of nine films, exemplify how a mask's distance, distillation, and duality can generate meaning. The Star Wars helmet-mask is a type of material character that can communicate a mixture of ideas, including conformity, emotional reserve, concealment, disguise, and transformation. The mask's potential in Star Wars is epitomized by Darth Vader, who sits at the center of two trilogies, and has inspired the villain for a third—Kylo Ren—who expands the mask's powers even further. The first live-action Star Wars streaming series demonstrated the enduring appeal of the helmet-mask with its titular characters in *The Mandalorian* and *The Book of Boba Fett*. And Vader's own story continues to be fleshed out further in live-action. In the streaming series *Obi-Wan Kenobi* (2022), a younger Vader's mask is cut open during battle, revealing flesh and material at the same time: actors Hayden Christensen and James Earl Jones's voices competing in oscillation out of the half-covered face. There seems to be no end to how this iconic mask can assert its storytelling powers.

References

Abrams, J.J., director. 2015. *Star Wars: Episode VII—The Force Awakens*. Lucasfilm Ltd.

Alexander, Julia. 2017. "Star Wars: The Last Jedi is Divisive, but Kylo Ren Shouldn't Be." *Polygon*. https://www.polygon.com/2017/12/18/16791400/star-wars-the-last-jedi-kylo-ren-adam-driver-spoilers.

Blumenthal, Eileen. 2005. *Puppetry: A World History*. New York, NY: Harry N. Abrams.

Burns, Kevin, director. 2007. *Star Wars: The Legacy Revealed*. Prometheus Entertainment, the History Channel.

Clark, Mark. 2015. *Star Wars FAQ: Everything Left to Know About the Trilogy That Changed the Movies*. Milwaukee, WI: Hal Leonard Corporation.

Evans, Nick. 2017. "Why Star Wars: The Last Jedi Made the Decision about Kylo Ren's Mask." *CinemaBlend*, December 26, 2017. https://www.cinemablend.com/news/1751099/why-star-wars-the-last-jedi-made-the-decision-about-kylo-rens-mask.

Johnson, Rian, director. 2017. *Star Wars: Episode VIII—The Last Jedi*. Lucasfilm.

Kershner, Irvin, director. 1980. *Star Wars: Episode V—The Empire Strikes Back*. Screenplay by Leigh Brackett and Lawrence Kasdan. Lucasfilm Ltd.

Lyne, Chris. 2019. "Complete Breakdown of the Entire Empire Magazine Article about 'Star Wars: The Rise of Skywalker.'" *Star Wars News Net*. https://www.starwarsnewsnet.com/2019/10/rise-skywalker-abrams-terrio-empire.html.

Millet, Lydia. 2002. "Becoming Darth Vader." In *A Galaxy Not So Far Away: Writers and Artists on Twenty-Five Years of Star Wars*, edited by Glenn Kenny. New York, NY: Henry Holt and Company.

Richau, Amy. 2018. "The Introduction of Kylo Ren and the Meaning of a Mask." *StarWars.com*. https://www.starwars.com/news/the-introduction-of-kylo-ren-and-the-meaning-of-a-mask.

Sunstein, Cass R. 2016. *The World According to Star Wars*. New York, NY: William and Morrow Publishers.

5
CLIMBING OUT OF THE SARLACC PIT

The Problematic Side of Material Character Powers

We've spent the last four chapters looking at the way material character powers have created meaning in some of the best live-action Star Wars stories. But material characters' unique powers can be used in negative ways as well, and in live-action Star Wars, they often perform a kind of Other-ness that can reflect, and even reinforce, negative tropes, representations, and stereotypes. This chapter unpacks how a combination of distance, distillation, and duality have engaged such negative patterns with Star Wars material characters. Divided into three sections, this chapter looks first at droids in service, followed by key examples of material character engagement with racial representation in Star Wars. The final section presents a hopeful trajectory: the way the first live-action Star Wars streaming series have wielded material character powers in ways that begin to counteract past harm.

Section 1: Droids in Service

C-3PO and R2-D2 introduced Star Wars' first audiences to a special kind of material character, the Star Wars droid, who would play in the gap between human and machine, pet and robot. C-3PO and R2-D2 were modeled after the protagonists of Akira Kurosawa's 1958 film *Hidden Fortress*: a pair of peasants who find themselves haplessly caught up in a war. Lucas borrowed the use of these characters in a number of ways; like *Hidden Fortress*, Star Wars begins by following the perspectives of its lowest-status characters. The droids are a distilled version of these peasants in terms of their powerlessness and social station—they are not just lowly humans; they are beneath humans: they are machines. They bring us into a galaxy with hierarchical structures that both reflect and extend those of the real world. Within the Star Wars stratum that

DOI: 10.4324/9781003137559-7

places humans above the non-human (the creature as pet, sidekick, beast, villain, or simply "scum") the droid occupies the lowest rung of all. The audience is oriented to this understanding, which isn't questioned (at least in the first two trilogies) but established and relied upon from the beginning of Star Wars. In his 1980 article, "Bergsonian Comedy and the Human Machine in 'Star Wars,'" Lane Roth analyzes the first (and at that time only) Star Wars film's projection of the droids within a larger social hierarchy as established by Obi-Wan Kenobi (Alec Guinness)'s description of Mos Eisley and its cantina bar, where they hope to hire a pilot:

> We are first introduced to this locale as a "wretched hive of scum and villainy," through Obe-Wan [sic] Kenobi's *caveat* to hero Luke Skywalker. We then see the interior of this infamous spot through contiguous shots which display the exotic and often hideous countenance of the clientele. Yet when the droids attempt to enter with Luke, the barkeep yells, "Hey, we don't serve their kind, here." The lines are clearly drawn: the repulsive and the criminal are tolerated, so long as they are life forms; discrimination is voiced only against machines.
>
> *(Roth 1980, 2)*

The strange cantina patrons may have been accepted at the bar, but they're still beneath regular people like Luke. The first Star Wars film set a precedent for acceptable prejudice against the non-human (in what would become its wider epic), as well as this hierarchy: humans sit at the top, creatures in the middle, droids at the bottom.

Though artificial intelligence is a real element of our world (and more so today than in the early days of Star Wars) the notion of a synthetic sentient being is still a fiction, and can only be performed in an arena of pretend, which adds to their compelling liminality and power as low-status characters who make meaning. The duality of real–fiction stands in their status as artificial, manufactured beings. The concept of the "robot" comes from theatre; it is rooted in the very notion of playacting. *Science Friday* producer Christopher Intagliata offers this helpful illumination of the term's history:

> As a word, *robot* is a relative newcomer to the English language. It was the brainchild of a brilliant Czech playwright, novelist and journalist named Karel Čapek (1880-1938) who introduced it in his 1920 hit play, *R.U.R.*, or *Rossum's Universal Robots*. *Robot* is drawn from an old Church Slavonic word, *robota*, for "servitude," "forced labor" or "drudgery." The word, which also has cognates in German, Russian, Polish and Czech, was a product of the central European system of serfdom by which a tenant's rent was paid for in forced labor or service.
>
> *(Intagliata 2011)*

Robots were associated from their earliest moment of fictional conception with service and free labor. Star Wars droids have a direct ancestorial tie to *R.U.R*: the play influenced Fritz Lang's 1927 *Metropolis* robot, Maschinenmensch (Nelson 2003, 260), a primary design inspiration for C-3PO.

As figures of performance who project an aspirational dream, robots connect fantasy as whimsy to fantasy as hoped-for reality: a future filled with artificial beings who can both please and serve people, and—because they are not "people"—won't require fair treatment or compensation, and might even replace those who do. The power of distance allows droids to operate like humans in any ways the story wishes them to without actually *being* humans. So, when the need arises for a disposable army, here is a figure that can be killed by the hundreds without mess or guilt (death and dismemberment of battle droids in the prequels are even played as physical comedy). In his video essay, *The Tragedy of Droids*, culture critic Jonathan McIntosh points to how Star Wars has historically left its galaxy's treatment of mechanical beings unquestioned, and how their ambiguity as living or not-living things means that some might have feelings that endear us to them—such as fear or affection—while others can be disposable machines, such as the battle droids (McIntosh 2020).

C-3PO and R2-D2 offer two contrasting examples of real-world service roles often portrayed in fiction. In building his droid's personality, Anthony Daniels created an upright posture that physicalized a highly formal, butler-type servant, making the droid quite literally rigid. C-3PO holds the duality of novel familiarity in his performance of that particular stock type, as well as the outward similarity to prior fictional robots in his design. This crossing between a high-end servant and a robot makes C-3PO fit with his station and primary directive: to serve his betters, and take pride in that role. R2-D2 represents another type of ideal servant: the surprisingly capable pet. The droid may not be cuddly, but he is objectively cute—much due to his designed child-like beeps and the way his head and body are often puppeteered to express stark emotions such as alarm or glee. R2 communicates in a way similar to Baby Yoda—his mechanical shaking when excited, rapid beeping when concerned, head turns when pensive—all of these distilled movements make him also puppy-like. Live-action Star Wars routinely puts this droid in a position to save the day at the last minute with an act of surprising capability, cleverness and/or self-sacrifice. R2 embodies a kind of conflation between the fantasy of the adorable animal who can do unexpected things, and an on-demand AI assistant. Luke's calls to R2 are not unlike commands that arrived in the real-world vernacular decades after his invention, such as "Hey Siri" and "Hey Alexa." These calls to disembodied friendly female servants function similarly to R2: they look up information, store and deliver messages, and (ideally) always respond when called. R2's distance from the human enables this pet-like service in its combination with the robot body. He looks like a vacuum cleaner, so while he may be Luke's little buddy, he is also his appliance. His looks, which are nowhere close to a human's, activate the power of distance to assist in disassociating him from our own kind. C-3PO and R2-D2, our host-bots in this galaxy far far away, are both conveniently alive in their behaviors, but only in ways beneficial to humans in the fiction, to its creators, and to the audience who may hope to enjoy their characterizations without worrying about their treatment.

To watch much of live-action Star Wars uncritically, we must on some level accept these metallic characters as less than human, beneath us, even while empathizing with their emotions, delighting in their personalities, and endearing ourselves to their adorable sensitivities. In other words: we're invited to accept them as human in every way but material makeup. However, live-action Star Wars storytelling did begin confronting this question of droid ethics with *Solo*'s L3-37 in 2018. L3 is not only the first live-action robot to challenge the status of her kind, but she's also the first principal female droid (nearly all droids are assigned a male gender as if by default). She makes an excellent case study for how material character powers are used in representing droid service—even in how her challenge ultimately fails—so I will here offer a more extended analysis of her character and function in the film.

Physically performed and voiced by actress-comedian Phoebe Waller-Bridge, L3 is humanoid but very clearly a machine—her face is closer to R2's than C-3PO's, her legs are hard metal, awkwardly ending in functional nobs at the bottom rather than feet. Her body contains tools, which she often pulls out to insert expertly into other machines. She is scrappy-looking, and when her head isn't working well, she'll give it a bang the way Han Solo hits the Millennium Falcon dashboard to get it working. L3 is a suit character enhanced by CGI, enabling her metal face and torso to replace the actor's in post-production. This hybridization lends L3 the kind of absent presence that's

FIGURE 5.1   The droid L3-37 in *Solo* (LUCASFILM)

successful in Anthony Daniel's portrayal of C-3PO from within the suit, and yet the distance from the human is here teased in replacing Waller-Bridge's neck and torso with wires. It looks as if no human being could possibly be inside—and yet her movements are grounded and believable, driven by the performer on set. L3's design is very much in sync with the Star Wars thing aesthetic—she looks like a hybrid droid, rigged from parts recycled from other droids; her awkward imperfections suggest a storied history. In fact, she was designed to be a "self-made woman, literally and figuratively," according to costume designer Glyn Dillon (Szostak 2018, 170). The design and performance also coalesce in a way that plays with the duality of limited limitlessness: L3 works within the constraints of what appears to be very tangible, almost primitive hardware. And though she is part CGI, L3 is grounded in the physical limitations of what the human actor can do.

As Star Wars' first significant female robot, L3 comes out swinging. Designed to be physically large, weighty, and strong, her image comports with her dialog: she may be a droid, but she walks and talks like a woman in charge of herself. She is outspoken, aggressive, and—significantly—capable of growth and change: she discovers her "true purpose" (Howard 2018) in the film as a droid abolitionist. We first meet her in a bar where droids are in a kind of fighting pit reminiscent of actual bot battles—calling for the droids to exercise free will and stand up against their exploitation. L3's distance from the human being allows situational comedy as she attempts to assert herself with young Lando Calrissian (Donald Glover), the human companion she serves as a co-pilot and whom she insists is not her master. The writers have situated the material characters in this way to point to their living-death duality: she and the other droids are understood to be not alive but suggestive of life restrained and unfulfilled as mere tools. This works at first because L3 and all other droids are set up as comic relief in the film. But L3's liminal status as a vibrantly alive and self-aware, rights-asserting machine gets exploited as the plot continues. Her material character powers are used in ways that undermine the potential for feminist messaging. An early clue to her fate comes when her *distance* from the humans, Lando and Han (Alden Ehrenreich), enable them to casually discuss her as an object. Lando explains to Han that the only reason he doesn't wipe her memory is because it contains such an outstanding navigational system, establishing that (1) he has the power to erase her mind and (2) he chooses not to, because her service to him is too valuable. L3 is a "she," as in a person with a gender, but she is also a useful piece of technology.

L3's comic frame encourages dismissiveness of serious issues this unique droid seems to embody as a material character in the climax of her brief story. That climax begins on the planet Kessel, a dreaded place filled with toiling droids and enslaved Wookiees, where L3 inadvertently starts a revolt. It's quite comic at first, as the droids dance around free à la *Wall-E*'s rogue robots, but once the Wookiees join the uprising against their jailers (themselves helmet-masked creatures called Pyke), the stakes feel higher. As L3 shouts to Lando that she's found her true purpose, and as she raises her metal hand triumphantly in the air—a clear gesture of resistance—a blaster strikes her metal body, knocking her to the ground. Lando dashes heroically into the fray to save her, managing to rescue only her head and torso. On the ship, Lando holds L3's remains as she dies in his arms with a mechanical sputtering and a human voice. He puts his forehead to her metal disk head and weeps. The humanity of her damaged body shutting down in Lando's grieving arms—remarkable in and of itself in suggesting such deep attachment between man and machine—is almost immediately undercut by what the humans do next. Lando and Han decide they need to take L3's "neural core" and put it into the ship's navigation system to save themselves. Their companion Qi'ra rips it out of the droid's body, uttering an apology, and they hook her up. The droid's brains work without her, apparently, and for much of the rest of the action sequence to follow, where Han is attempting to pilot the Falcon out of trouble, Lando reads what "she" is telling them to do with those remarkable navigating skills he mentioned earlier. L3's voice is silenced, reduced to a panel of lights (like a GPS screen) which the humans use as a map for escape. Perhaps this would have felt better with a different droid, one who is service-oriented in personality, sad as that still may have been. But L3 is the opposite. And this action is treated in the film, if not by the characters (who do act momentarily sad about it), as a fairly fun and light turn of events—the plot quickly moves on to chase sequences and the rest of the human story.

L3's characterization within the *Solo* plot, particularly in how her "life" ends or is permanently incorporated into service inside a larger machine, is problematic not only in how it undercuts the challenge made to the ethics of droid service/slavery the film proposes (a first in live-action Star Wars) but in how it aligns the first significant female droid with servitude. Many critics and fans noted the problems with L3 and her unfulfilled potential. Some connected it to wider entertainment tropes. In his article "'Solo' Droid L3-37 Is the First Woke Bot of 'Star Wars,'" Spencer Kornhaber reflects on this choice within a larger context of L3's pop-culture contemporaries as well as the AI in our own world:

> popular culture of late has gone beyond the sci-fi assumption that artificial intelligence will one day pass the Turing test to ask whether, once bots can think like people, they'll deserve ethical consideration like people do. Is it wrong to mistreat a being like Dolores from *Westworld*, and can an entity like Janet from *The Good Place* feel happiness, even if both aren't technically human? It's likely no coincidence that such thought experiments have been centered around putatively female characters, as seen in the examples above as well as in *Ex Machina, Her,* and now *Solo*.

The fact that real-world helper bots like Apple's Siri or Amazon's Alexa tend to be programmed as "women" may be rooted in the sexist belief that secretarial work is female.

(Kornhaber 2018)

Again, just before she's shot, L3 joyfully pronounces that freedom-fighting is her "true purpose"—but her fate reveals what her real *purpose* is: to serve the needs of the men. Her material character powers assist this conscription: because she is distanced from a human being, the ripping out of her brains from her body is only slightly violent, not gruesome (Qi'ra's apology is rather comically played), and the living-death duality means that the material character that is her metal corpse isn't dead, it's just awaiting further service, and can be repurposed. Her intangible talents are distilled into one piece of her internal gadgetry, the piece of her most useful to the humans. Her talent is conscripted into perennial service to the men who pilot the Millennium Falcon, who will pass their ownership of "her" back and forth between them. L3's distance is convenient to the *Solo* story because it enables several roles as a not-person: comic revolutionary, the butt of jokes, and GPS system all rolled into one.

Like C-3PO, R2, and other Star Wars droids, L3 carries ethical complications in her very being as a service bot. The fact that her story undermines her potential is itself a message, that material character powers can generate negative as well as positive meaning. Whether conscripted into service to the plot, or within it, fictional robots reflect larger cultural systems of social hierarchy and labor. As material characters, robots hold a special liminal status in our fictions, and present opportunities unique to their type of material character.

Section 2: Racial Representation

Material characters are often used for negative representations of race, reinforcing harmful stereotypes in a range of media—from small puppet shows to big-screen movies. In Star Wars, there has always been concern about the lack of diversity among the human characters, and some critics have argued that aliens represent the harmful notion of the racialized, colonized, and/or subjugated Other. This section begins by establishing how several Star Wars material characters have expressed harmful stereotypes before exploring three specific topics: the absent presence of Asian characters in live-action Star Wars, the lost opportunities in Jar Jar Binks, and the helmet-masks' participation in racial representation.

Criticisms of Star Wars for Racial Stereotypes

Chapter 4 analyzed the revelation of a human face beneath Vader's mask in *Episode VI: Return of the Jedi* as a material character moment clearly intended to redeem a villain's humanity. But there are other interpretations of this meaningful scene. When Luke removes Vader's black face mask, it reveals the white face of actor Sebastian Shaw. Theatre and cinema scholar Kevin J. Wetmore reads this in the uncovering of Vader's face: "when he is no longer bad, he is no longer black" (Wetmore 2005)—referring to the fact that he is voiced by James Earl Jones up until that final moment in his story. Jones is one of only a very small number of actors of color included in the original trilogy (his voice is a presence inside absence). Wetmore's interpretation of this scene is part of his larger view into the way the first two Star Wars trilogies used the non-human to represent the Other inside a white-centered story. In his 2005 book *The Empire Triumphant: Race, Religion, and Rebellion in the Star Wars Films*, Wetmore analyzes the first two trilogies, finding that its heroes, "Luke, Han, Obi-Wan and Anakin—are all white males who achieve victory and dominance over their (often alien) adversaries with the assistance of subservient Others", putting the white man at the center of Star Wars (Wetmore 2005). Wetmore interprets the role of the non-human characters in his analysis, and suggests that "people of color of the Star Wars universe are literally alienated—they are represented as aliens, as complete and utterly non-human. For the most part in the two trilogies, non-white means non-human. They are alienated from human psychology by literally being aliens" (Wetmore 2005).

Many other viewers and critics saw problematic racial representations in characters at the time of the films' releases, particularly after the first prequel film, *Episode I: The Phantom Menace*. One of the most notable responses was Eric Harrison's 1999 *Los Angeles Times* article "A Galaxy Far, Far Off Racial Mark?" which addressed the overwhelming fan complaints about racial stereotypes in Jar Jar and other CGI characters. Harrison compiled a range of responses for the article, and in it, he considers the larger context of Lucas's historical approach to diversity in creatures and droids, but not in humans:

> some viewers have found his handling of race problematic since he released the first "Star Wars" movie in 1977. Grousers privately noted that the movie had Wookies [sic], robots, jazz-playing aliens and— inexplicably in this far-off galaxy—white people who spoke with British accents. But nowhere on screen were there humanoids with non-pink skin.
>
> *(Harrison 1999)*

One of Harrison's most important points is that the existence of a range of creatures and droids generates a particularly negative meaning in the context of a made-up galaxy where white-ness is the human norm.

Wetmore analyzes Star Wars characters as part of American entertainment history, and considers how several acutely reflect harmful stereotypes of African Americans:

> Jar Jar and the Gungun [sic] are what Hal Foster terms 'exclusionary stereotypes,' an effective way to turn the Other into 'a pure object, spectacle, [or] clown.' ... in the second trilogy, blacks are reduced to the clown figure of Jar Jar, the servant Panaka, and the purposeless Mace Windu. In Reddick's formulation, Jar Jar is 'the mental inferior' 'the happy slave,' and 'the irresponsible citizen.' ... He is clumsy, a coward, and simple-minded, but devoted to Qui-Gon, Anakin, and Amidala as a happy slave would be.
> *(Wetmore 2005)*

Wetmore sources African American history scholar Lawrence Reddick's designated nineteen Black stereotypes in film, as summarized by Richard A. Maynard, as well as writings by art critic Hal Foster, to support his arguments about the wider context Star Wars' use of stereotypes in the prequel trilogies. American film historian Donald Bogle's work also offers evidence for Wetmore's connections between Jar Jar and the "coon" trope, and it helps underscore its dangers. He explains how Bogle "defines a 'coon' as 'the Negro as amusement object and black buffoon,' and posits it as 'the most blatantly degrading of all black stereotypes'" (Wetmore 2005). Bringing these and other writers' work to bear on Star Wars character analysis, Wetmore lays out the overwhelming parallels between features of the "coon" trope and other racial stereotypes, in Jar Jar's design, characteristics, dialect, dialog, actions, and relationships to the action of the film. The comparisons leave no room for doubt as to the character's presentation of these caricatures. A similar argument can be made (and has been) about other non-human characters in Star Wars, most especially those appearing in the prequel trilogy. Well-supported criticisms relating to negative racial representation in Star Wars—particularly non-humans—abound in Wetmore's study, in other academic writing, and in wider fandom.

For the scope of this study, my inquiry is this: how do material character powers contribute to negative representations of race in live-action Star Wars? I find that a look at the absent presence of Asian characters in the prequels offers an important perspective and way-in to establish a wider context within live-action Star Wars, particularly the prequels. I follow this with an analysis of Jar Jar's lost potential, and a closer look at how helmet-mask troopers intersect with racial representation.

The Absent Presence of Asian Characters

By sourcing a variety of world cultural images, traditions, designs, and even religious beliefs, Star Wars has often crossed the line from inspiration to appropriation. This problem is particularly acute and ironic when it comes to Star Wars sources from the Asian continent, so I focus on this specifically (for a more in-depth study, I recommend Chapter 5 of Wetmore's *The Empire Triumphant*). Although there are very few Asian humans in his two trilogies, Asian-derived images, names, and concepts inspired George Lucas from the beginning. They are particularly present and problematic in the prequel trilogy, which included design choices, dialects, and names derived from Asian cultures as well as Asian cultural stereotypes. A group of CGI material characters called Neimoidians are especially concerning. Writing for the academic blog *Contemporary Racism,* D. Adamczak describes how these semi-humans were

> metaphorically ripped to shreds for being obvious representations of Eastern Asian stereotypes. This is not only due to the clothing they wear, being long tunics, similar to those seen in historical depictions of Chinese royalty, but also due to the quick, stunted way in which the aliens communicate in English. This quick, stunted way of speaking is often used to further racist stereotypes of how people from Eastern Asia present themselves when attempting to speak in English or interact in American culture.
>
> *(Adamczak 2019)*

These material characters, who project negative qualities (greed, gullibility, disingenuousness), use mock-Asian-sounding dialects to speak English. The Jedi "good guys" they interact with display positive qualities (politeness, wisdom, bravery) and are white-presenting human men who speak English with British accents. So much of the Asian presence in the prequels comes in the form of cultural appropriation and material characters who present racial caricatures in this context.

The duality of real-fiction participates in the way the power of material characters like the Neimoidians radiates beyond Star Wars. Some critics have suggested that these stereotypes encourage racist fans who have objected to Disney's casting non-white humans in significant roles. *Guardian* critic Ben Child (referencing the later sequel films) refers to "certain so-called fans [who] balk at the prospect of seeing black men or Asian women flying the new movies' X-wings, but have no issue at all with syntactically challenged, green-skinned, giant-eared Jedi homunculi or oversized dog-faced teddy bear sidekicks" (Child 2021). Reflecting on the lasting influence of the prequels, Child suggests those earlier films did a poor job of attempting a cultural mix, and that this may have "accidentally ended up warming the cockles for modern-day Nazi Star Wars fans..." (Child 2021). Indeed, there may be a direct line between the appropriation of Asian cultures in Star Wars designs and creature creations, exacerbated by outright stereotypes, and anti-Asian attitudes among Star Wars fans that reared up particularly acutely a decade and a half later. After appearing in *Episode VIII: The Last Jedi* (2017), actor Kelly Marie Tran was famously subjected to a torrent of racist trolling. The real-world consequences of her treatment may not be so surprising after decades of stories where the heroes are overwhelmingly white, the few humans acted by people of color are ancillary to the action, and so many non-human or semi-human characters perform racial and cultural stereotypes.

The inclusion of Asian-derived aesthetics, coupled with the relative paucity of Asian characters in live-action Star Wars' first two trilogies, engages the dualities of absent presence and real-fiction in ways that extend beyond the material characters and into the films themselves, as well as the world of fandom. These material character powers affect the larger experience of Star Wars, underscoring how they can participate in negative meaning-making in response to the present and historical context of how the epic's casting and characterizations are managed.

The Lost Potential of Jar Jar

Notwithstanding the liberal appropriation of various cultures throughout the prequel trilogy, it appears that Lucasfilm did not intend to create such disturbing caricatures in figures like Watto and Jar Jar Binks. But Lucas himself has argued that it is important to take responsibility for the outcome and meaning of one's artwork (Wheat 2000); such reflective critique is critical. What follows here is an analysis of Jar Jar not as a representative case study of racially problematic Star Wars characters, but as the lightning rod he is for so much of the essential pushback *Phantom* in particular has received. If the Star Wars creators did not intend for Jar Jar to be a racial stereotype, and yet he so clearly is one, then how did it happen? There are many possible reasons for this, all worth examining. Here is my question: did the fact that he was an animated, made-up creature worsen the stereotypes he projected? I believe it did. Here we'll unpack how distance, distillation, and several of the dualities helped make this material character harmful.

Jar Jar's distance from the human being opens up a range of creative possibilities for what he might have looked like. Inspiration for the character's design came from a range of sources, including frogs, ducks, and humans. The sculpture of his head was based on concept designs by Terryl Whitlatch, who drew on her knowledge of animal anatomy to detail his interior muscle and skeletal structure (Salisbury 2018, 85). Jar Jar mostly appears on screen via CGI animation as a floppy-eared combination of a tall human and cartoonish amphibian with large legs, a wide mouth, and eyes that pop over his head like a crab's. On set, Jar Jar was performed by actor and dancer Ahmed Best; his movements and interactions inspired the final outcome of the fully-animated Jar Jar, whose voice Best also performed.

While material characters designed as a combination of different types of animals can result in a very imaginative participant in a story, the danger lies in making a character a semi-human, particularly if that character is to be the butt of jokes. In *Episode I: The Phantom Menace*, Jar Jar is introduced as the comic foil for the human protagonists (Obi-Wan, Qui-Gon, Anakin, and Padme), who are all white. Material characters routinely bring comic relief and levity to stories—it's an important material character function in Star Wars—but Jar Jar has entire comic *bits* centered around his clumsiness and animalistic tendencies. For example, he uses his tongue to retrieve fruit at the dinner table in *Phantom* like a frog, prompting a stern, parental warning from the well-mannered Jedi Master Qui-Gon (Liam Neeson). Distance also enables distillation, which makes the stereotypes burn brighter. When Jar Jar's extra-long tongue falls out of his mouth after he accidentally electrocutes himself in that same film, the "bit" presents him as the essence of a buffoon. Because he is a speaking, bipedal being, Jar Jar is similar to humans in posture and in some parts of his characterization, but decidedly another category of creature—a figure of low status because his culture and his physical makeup are *unlike* the dominant, civilized species of heroes like Padme (Natalie Portman) and Anakin (Jake Lloyd). His distance from the human being moves to a point of alienation and enhances that sense of social distance and status because, as an improbable-looking CGI character, he appears out of place in their live-action world. Having a CGI character perform in live-action isn't itself a problem, but when exaggerated characteristics underscore how impossibly different he is from Obi-Wan and Padme, for example, it widens the human-creature line between him and the human species.

Jar Jar's duality of novel familiarity emerges out of this distance as well and further supports the stereotypes he projects. Jar Jar was novel in his appearance in 1999 as an entirely made-up creature, but many fans and critics were disturbed by the performance of familiar racial tropes in Jar Jar, the Gungans, and other non-human or semi-human characters. Wetmore calls his dialog

FIGURE 5.2   Jar Jar and the Jedi in *The Phantom Menace* (LUCASFILM)

and accent "reflective of the dialect of blacks found in nineteenth century minstrel shows and in more recent representations of blacks such as the various manifestations of *Amos and Andy* and *Gone with the Wind*" and echoes what many critics have clocked as "stereotypical dialect for Caribbean characters" (Wetmore). Such negative familiarity seemed ludicrously off-the-mark to Lucas at the time. Journalist Alynda Wheat documented his vehement denial of racist stereotypes in *Phantom* in her conversation with the filmmaker in 2000 (Wheat 2000). In his *Los Angeles Times* article, Harrison cites a Lucasfilm spokesperson arguing that the *Phantom* characters' distance from the actual world renders any associations with reality preposterous:

> Lynne Hale, a spokeswoman for Lucasfilm, called such interpretations "absurd." "There is nothing in 'Star Wars' that is racially motivated," she said in a statement. "'Star Wars' is a fantasy movie set in a galaxy far, far away. It is populated with humans, aliens, creatures, droids, robots and other fantastic creatures …. To dissect this movie as if it has a direct reference to the world that we know today is absurd."
>
> *(Harrison 1999)*

Yet Star Wars is undeniably part of a long history of reflecting the world we live in through science fiction and fantasy.

The duality of absent presence intersects with this familiar novelty and the larger context of Star Wars casting practices. Actor Ahmed Best was one of only a few actors of color in any Star Wars film up to and including *The Phantom Menace* in 1999, and he was hidden. The hiding alone isn't the problem—absent presence is a duality of the material character—except that it *is* a problem in this franchise where there are so few visible humans of color. Another part of the context adding to the harmful meaning is that racial stereotypes are a go-to for animated characters in the prequels in general, not just Jar Jar and the Gungans. D. Adamczak suggests that "instead of using their imagination to envision new forms of life and creatures whose biology and societal norms are fascinating and intriguing, the creators simply opted to take racist stereotypes" and "place these stereotypes within alien bodies" (Adamczak 2019). Harrison writes of *Phantom*, "Different racial groups were represented by aliens, much like those old cartoons that used animals as stand-ins for racial groups" (Harrison 1999). That connection to "old cartoons" actually goes even further. Much early animation in the United States drew from Blackface minstrelsy (Richards 2019).

In a 2015 interview, Ahmed Best described Jar Jar's creation process positively, as emerging from "a symbiotic relationship between the animators, the software designers, and the actor," and talked about how he drew inspiration in his Jar Jar movement approach from Buster Keaton and Charlie Chaplin (Godfrey and Novi 2015). Here we engage the duality of absent presence:

Best's efforts as a performer were parsed out—Jar Jar had his voice, and the animated character was inspired by his movements, but there was misalignment in the characterization within the film. Jar Jar was not situated in the story in such a way as to support an empathetic clown characterization, which requires thoughtful context. Jar Jar is a side gag and obstacle to the heroes, and the film never lingers on his point-of-view as a powerless character the way it does with C-3PO and R2 in the original trilogy. And Jar Jar's cartoon antics are ungrounded and buffoonish, in part because he is, in fact, a cartoon. Physical comedy derives much of its power from encounters with external obstacles, but Jar Jar's interactions with "real" objects in *Phantom* appear artificial and therefore hard to credit. When he accidentally juggles some objects in Anakin's house due to his clumsiness, there is no real gravity for him to work against or to create credible stakes; the things he's dropping are not real, so nothing bad will happen if they fall. Of course, cartoon characters can be very funny when stumbling over objects in a world where everything is animated, but that's not what *Phantom* is. Much of the film's environs are rendered by CGI, but the story-driving characters are played by flesh-and-blood actors in locations that are supposed to match their own convincing presence. This is live-action, so the absence of an actor who modeled the movement in this case, poorly contextualized, contributed to its failures and to the degrading of a potentially interesting new Star Wars character.

The duality of real-fiction means that Jar Jar's influence as a harmful trope, unfortunately, has significant real-world reach. Jar Jar was aggressively marketed for children's play. Mini-Jar Jars flooded stores in 1999 as action figures and other tangible merch. Jar Jar may be made up, but he is also a real thing with real impact: Star Wars is highly influential and serves as cultural education, particularly for children (Wetmore 2005).

There are many reasons for Jar Jar's problematic characterizations. What his material character status contributes to the caricature is useful to unpack via the ways distance, distillation, and several dualities worked within the context of his presentation and contextualization in *The Phantom Menace*. Jar Jar is an animal-like humanoid that emerged with the potential for interesting creature design but was ultimately rendered, written, and used as a sub-human cartoon with exaggerated negative attributes aligned with the "coon" trope. He presents a distilled, and yet disguised (novel), presentation of racial (recognizable) stereotypes further supported and reinforced by his dialog, dialect, relationships, actions, and situations. Duality of absent presence also held the potential for a talented performer to create a new kind of Star Wars character through his physical impulses and choices, but the final performance of a CGI cartoon was ultimately too far removed from the actor, and too poorly used. The real-fiction duality plays out in the harm this fictional character has created, not only through tangible replications of his body as toys but in cultural education and perpetuation (in some ways in hiding behind his materiality), of harmful messages. I may join other fans and scholars in wondering if there were any way this character might have been handled differently—and of course, there were many ways. Looking both backward and forwards, it is critical that filmmakers know the history of racial representations, stereotypes, and tropes in art and entertainment, including awareness of how they perpetuate harm. Working with material characters is an act of presentation and representation, so understanding how they wield power is essential, particularly when constructing a character who is to be laughed at, and especially if they are going to be close to human, but not quite. Finally, context itself presents the meaning—where there is already a problem of parity, disparaging presentations of Other-ness, and/or white-centeredness, material characters will radiate meaning in relationship to it. Even the most powerful and well-drawn character cannot counteract these core problems.

Beneath the Helmet-Mask

In live-action Star Wars, the helmet-mask holds unique powers to enact separation and violence through the power of distance. This section investigates how helmet-masks in live-action Star Wars troopers intersect with racial representation via the clones, debuted in the prequel films, and Star Wars' first Black stormtrooper, performed by John Boyega in *Episode VII: The Force Awakens*.

Chapter 1 looked at how the prequels' use of CGI engendered identical clone trooper characters. Temuera Morrison performs Jango Fett, a galactic mercenary and the clones' genetic donor. Morrison appears for the first time in *Episode II: Attack of the Clones* as one of only a few humans of color, and his face is multiplied via CGI technology into the hundreds. The same is done with actor Daniel Logan—who, like Morrison, is a New Zealander of native Māori descent—playing the young Boba Fett and face of younger clones. Some fans at the time interpreted this as a positive direction for more diverse representation. The Nerds of Color pop culture blog's editor, Keith Chow, wrote a 2018 article called "Go Asians: a History of AAPI Representation in Star Wars" where he suggests Morrison's identity as a Māori means that the clones, including characters like Captain Cody, would be "coded as Pacific Islander" (Chow 2018).

Though Boba Fett is fully developed as a character decades later in the *The Book of Boba Fett* (which I analyze in the next section of this chapter), Jango and the clones mainly function in the prequels to serve the story from the side, and they offer some problematic presentations. In *Episode II: Attack of the Clones*, the titular soldiers are dispatched into battle in full armor, including helmet-masks, which make them appear similar to the iconic stormtroopers from the original trilogy, and emphasize the sense of faceless sameness.

Like all masks, these helmets create a degree of distance from the exposed human: we cannot read their expressions, their faces are identical (and in this case, we know them to be identical even *under* the mask). The story of the prequels presents the clones as less than human, even machine-like in that they are genetically designed beings "altered" and programmed through their factory upbringing to fight obediently. The helmet-masked clones in the prequels thereby function as both semi-humans and concealed humans. Their almost machine-like status is reinforced by these uniform helmet-masks that hide any subtle human differences between them, their feelings, and their similarity to we humans in the audience. And like all helmet-masked soldiers in live-action Star Wars, they also take the majority of the blaster fire. They are in this way similar to the battle droids, the rather silly CGI material character soldiers the clones fight in the prequels. Material character distance, for all of Star Wars's fighting droids and masked soldiers, enables this violence to conveniently play out without overtly stimulating the audience to consider their individuality or feelings; there isn't significant evidence in the prequels that the clones have either.

In addition to facilitating violence, the clone troopers' degree of distance from humans (both as presented in the fiction, and in their concealment behind masks) enables the characters to separate from themselves when they remove the helmets, symbolizing a vacillation between their status as individual humans and identical, mass-produced military tools. The film does not seem to question the way the good-guy Jedi Knights direct these genetically engineered, programmed human beings to fight and die for them. The Jedi who oversee them, mainly Anakin (Hayden Christensen) and Obi-Wan Kenobi (Ewan McGregor), are white men, while the clones are concealed brown men, many of whom die in their service. Morrison's appearance in 2002's *Episode II: Attack of the Clones* was significant in that it brought the presence of a member of the global majority more fully into the story, and there was, as Chow suggests, a radiation outward from this choice given how many characters would carry Morrison's face. But there is also this: the clones are presented in the story as semi-humans who are grown and programmed, conscripted into forced service without choice or free will, and rendered disposable in battle. None of this is presented as concerning in the films. They have brown faces in a galaxy where most humans (and most humans who are in charge) are white. They loyally serve the good guys without question or challenge, and they all look alike.

The narrative as well as casting choices in the later sequel trilogy are more self-reflective about the dehumanizing of the masked trooper and the galaxy's lack of diversity. The first film's much-anticipated trailers feature John Boyega's face filling the screen as it emerges from a stormtrooper suit. In 2014, this seemed to promise the appearance of Star Wars' first live-action Black stormtrooper, and Boyega's presence in marketing materials suggested he'd be a figure of significance. The character's revelation in the trilogy was certainly significant, for a number of reasons, and takes advantage of the power of the mask. It takes place near the beginning of *Episode VII: The Force Awakens*, when a stormtrooper falls injured during a battle on the planet Jakku, and perspective shifts to focus on the fallen soldier and his companion's efforts to tend to him. This is a break in habit of live-action Star Wars, which had not to date taken narrative interest in the thoughts and feelings of its stormtroopers. The injured trooper reaches up to touch his companion's masked face, smearing it with blood as he dies. Marked with red fingerprints, the surviving soldier (later named Finn) staggers up and looks around, seemingly disoriented or perhaps experiencing an awakening. The camera stays on him as he whips his head around at the sight of troopers slaughtering villagers. When the marked trooper rejoins his regiment later, as part of a firing squad ordered to execute the remaining locals, he stands out visually because of the bloody handprint on his mask. This is a remarkable and meaningful symbol given the bloodlessness of trooper deaths in past live-action Star Wars (McIntosh 2020). He then stands out because of his actions: as his identical companions beside him raise up their guns, this soldier lowers his. The simple movement, paired with the handprint, communicates in the visual-gestural language of the material character to signal that in this story, stormtroopers experience humanity.

Once back on his ship, the marked stormtrooper removes his helmet to reveal his anguished face. The masked character's distance allows for this separation and, in this case (as with Vader), revelation. This is the first live-action stormtrooper to show its human face (the clones had exposed faces, but not these stormtroopers, who are presented as enslaved humans, not clones). In his video essay, *The Stormtrooper Paradox*, McIntosh argues that these two scenes are groundbreaking:

> The removal of a mask to expose someone's true humanity is a recurring motif in the Star Wars series, and we've seen hundreds if not thousands of stormtroopers before, but we've never seen one with a face. Both of these scenes communicate that under their iconic armor, stormtroopers are people, people with feelings and who feel pain both physically [and] emotionally.
>
> *(McIntosh 2020 transcript; punctuation is author's)*

The helmet-mask plays a critical role in enacting this reversal, or potential rectification, of how soldiers are treated in Star Wars. Moreover, this mask removal is doubly meaningful because at the same moment it humanizes the idea of the trooper, it reveals that the one to make this change might also prove to be Star Wars' first Black protagonist (the first two trilogies included Black characters in supportive positions, but the heroes were consistently white).

This moment of material character performance, which enacts these two "firsts" together, is meaningful beyond the screen. In the real world of 2015, John Boyega was simultaneously celebrated as a new-generation Star Wars hero and subjected to racist backlash. Finn's participation in the stories moved away from its center as the trilogy progressed: Rey and Kylo ultimately take up the romantic tension and nuanced relationship established between Rey and Finn in *Force Awakens*. Finn's initial promise as a lightsaber-wielding, complex Black hero goes unfulfilled.

Finn also intersects with another trooper character who challenges parity issues in Star Wars: Phasma (Gwendoline Christie), live-action Star Wars' first female trooper. In *The Last Jedi*, Finn is no longer masked, but his former overseer, Phasma, has never been seen without hers—we have only heard her commanding, British-sounding, clearly female voice emitting from a shiny gold helmet atop a matching suit. In their climactic duel, Phasma's mask breaks, and she falls into a pit. For a brief moment before she dies, the injured Phasma looks up at Finn with a single human eye peeking through a crack in her mask. The revelation of a half-face utilizes the duality of absent presence: her humanity is partly exposed by the actor's left eye, while the right is still covered by the material mask that frames her face. Phasma's distance, as a material character, enables her to almost separate from the person beneath, but not quite. This violation of the mask (a first in live-action Star Wars) enables the organic and material visage to share custody of the face, revealing her potential humanity and her villain-mask at the same time. Finn's reaction in that moment further ignites his humanity as well, suggesting surprise and perhaps momentary empathy, a crack in the relationship of two mortal enemies. Yet Phasma's death also represents an end (at least for the trilogy) to what the Star Wars creators seemed to dangle by turning a significant trooper character female: she was not the first of many female stormtroopers after all, but remained the only one of her kind in the trilogy (there is a masked woman in the next film, but no other troopers). As characters who used masks to conceal and reveal, Finn and Phasma begin with the powers of the material character both to advance the story and begin to offer race and gender parity in this historically white-male-dominated franchise. The idea of stormtroopers' humanity extended a little bit; a female Black ex-trooper named Jannah (Naomi Ackie) is introduced in *Episode IX: The Rise of Skywalker*, but the promise offered by that mask revelation—of more ethical exploration of the dehumanized soldier and centralizing heroes of color—isn't fully explored in the sequel trilogy.

Considering the absent presence of Asian characters, Jar Jar's problematic characterization, and the face-mask interactions of the troopers, reveals specific ways material character powers participate in harmful racial representation. When designed and/or performed in ways that further toxic tropes, material characters can be particularly potent in preserving, reproducing, and transferring their dangers. As we see with characters like Finn and Phasma, there is great opportunity in material character power to directly confront negative fictional and real-world patterns, though they require supportive stories to fulfill that potential. And there is hope in this direction: the first Star Wars live-action streaming series offer examples of how creative teams can better wield material character powers and consider the importance of the storytelling context in which they perform.

Section 3: A New Hope for Positive Material Character Representation

Decision-makers behind later live-action Star Wars answered the call for more diversity in creative leadership and casting. *Rogue One* was, in 2016, the first live-action Star Wars film to feature a cast composed predominantly of people of color, and notably featured a number of Asian actors in significant roles. The multi-episode streaming series launched in late 2019 (and continuing to this writing) are directed by a diverse range of talents, including Taika Waititi, Carl Weathers, and Deborah Chow. Most of the series' titular roles to date are performed by representatives of the global majority, including Pedro Pascal (*The Mandalorian*) and Diego Luna (*Andor*) with major characters like Fennec Shand (Ming-Na Wen) and Asoka (Rosario Dawson) performed by women of color. Particularly noteworthy, in this material character analysis, is how the rise in the status and complexity of material characters coincides with improved representation in the creative teams and actors. The titular heroes of the first two series, *The Mandalorian* and *The Book of Boba Fett*, are both helmet-mask characters, and the first series puts a puppet at the heart of its story.

In Chapter 1, I considered how the Disney+ streaming series began in 2019 and the early 2020s by turning back towards the original trilogy for characters, situations, and locations, with a hard leaning into elements of the Star Wars thing aesthetic. Picking up in the story timeline following *Episode VI: Return of the Jedi* from the 1980s, we see the old-school creatures who populated the cantina and Jabba's castle in the original Star Wars film now take up speaking roles. *Mandalorian* producers Dave Filoni and Jon Favreau were excited to flesh out stories for the minor characters that kids of their generation played with in action-figure miniature. The first two series that launched this transition to long-form, episodic live-action Star Wars would indeed move the frame to put these side-characters in the center—those that had been previously sidelined would now have their stories told (created) and in some cases with greater dignity and sensitivity to the need for Star Wars to reconsider and repair its past representations. In part because of the long-form storytelling (a movie is restricted to a few hours, while an episodic series can be any length), minor characters have more screen time—here they get full names and jobs.

Droids and creatures who served as extras in the original trilogy get in front of the camera much longer, and we learn more about them. The smelting droid who tortures his kind in Jabba's dungeon is promoted to above-stairs butler in *The Book of Boba Fett* (just as awkward and funny as it sounds) and a cousin to the Rancor monster from *Return of the Jedi* gets introduced as a gentle pet before dominating the final battle scene like an extra angry King Kong. But there is even more significant meaning in the way the two series re-draw two intersecting material characters (one an individual, and one a group) from the original and prequel trilogies: the masked Boba Fett and the Tusken Raiders.

For those less familiar with Boba Fett, I offer this summary of his live-action Star Wars appearances. The bounty hunter has a minor but vital role in the original trilogy (performed by Jeremy Bulloch). He is always masked and speaks only briefly. Introduced in *Episode V: The Empire Strikes Back* as one of several bounty hunters referred to as "scum" by an Imperial officer, Boba is a mercenary who hires himself out to Darth Vader to lay a trap for Luke. He ultimately flies away with the carbonite-encased Han Solo, delivering him to Jabba the Hutt for bounty. The effort to rescue Han is what brings Leia, Luke, Lando, C-3PO, and R-2 to Jabba's castle at the top of *Episode VI: Return of the Jedi*. At the climax of the battle to save Han, Boba fights on the side of Jabba, as they hover over the Sarlacc monster, a material character situated in a pit recessed inside the desert floor. Boba Fett falls into the Sarlacc pit along with other unfortunates during the fight, so he is presumed dead. There was a lot of fan buzz about this undignified end, for Boba Fett has always been one of the most popular Star Wars characters, in spite of his minor role in the films. Surely this is at least partly attributable to a toy manufacturing snafu: his 1980s action figure came with launching rockets later recalled as a choking hazard, making it one of the most coveted and expensive Star Wars collectibles of all time. But his popularity may also be due to his quiet mystique as the only significant masked figure in the original trilogy who had his own look, his own tools, and his own voice, other than Vader. He appeared in the original trilogy as the scruffy version of its slick villain, his dented helmet and chipped-paint armor asking as many questions as his concealed face.

The prequel film *Episode II: Attack of the Clones* re-introduces Boba Fett as a child, the adopted son of mercenary Jango Fett, who supplies genetic material for the clone army. Daniel Logan performs the role of an "unaltered" clone, a younger genetic equivalent of his adopted father/donor, Jango. This elevates the minor character in the epic story, giving Boba a more consequential role, a face, and a significant backstory as a child. Four decades later, a middle-aged Boba is reintroduced in the second season of *The Mandalorian,* in a way that would pose dramatic questions to be answered in his own titular series to follow, *The Book of Boba Fett* (2022).

Boba's surprise appearance in *The Mandalorian* (set at a time after his presumed death) presents the bounty hunter as an unmasked warrior in a way that brings greater meaning to his story, and better honors the actor and character's combined representational resonance in live-action Star Wars. In the second season of *The Mandalorian*, Boba appears in the first episode as a maskless man standing in the desert. He is identifiable by his face (that of the appropriately aged actor Temuera Morrison) which had belonged to the clone-donor Jango Fett (Boba's genetic donor), and all of the clone troopers. When he appears again in the second episode, audiences get a better look: indeed, he is not only maskless, everything about him is transformed. His whole head is naked and scarred, his hard, iconic armor replaced with soft cloth robes, his flame thrower and blaster substituted by a sculpted wooden stick. In that first significant Boba scene, this mysterious version of the bounty hunter from the original trilogy has little time to introduce himself to the masked Din Djarin (aka "Mando") before they are forced to collaborate on defeating a swarm of stormtroopers. Boba uses that wooden staff to take the troopers down with his impressive, almost acrobatic combat skills, dispatching them one or two at a time, his exposed face crinkling with effort and verve. This long-concealed character proves a highly capable and emotionally expressive person who does not need the armor and mask to fight and survive. Though the younger Jango and Boba both appeared with exposed faces at times in the prequels, they were also minor characters who shared those faces with hundreds of semi-humans. Here, Morrison's character is more set apart, he is a unique and (very) autonomous human being. Later in this same stormtrooper fight scene, when Boba has recovered and donned his iconic armor and helmet-mask, he faces down a second wave of adversaries with his suit's impressive gadgetry (flame thrower, rockets), making for a spectacular second act in this battle between two masked men and a group of stormtroopers. In this two-part fight scene, Boba Fett demonstrates first, in his hand-to-hand combat skill and staff-wielding, that technology does not make the man, and begs curiosity about who that man is. The fact that he has spent decades as a masked figure, and is now so fully exposed, deepens his mystery.

How this absence of the mask participates in Boba's character growth is as meaningful as Vader's has been to live-action Star Wars storytelling. The relationship between Boba the iconic masked figure from the 1980s and early 2000s, and Boba as a fully-realized protagonist for the 2020s, is explored more deeply in *The Book of Boba Fett*. And the series answers the question posed by his earlier surprise appearance in *The Mandalorian*: how did he get out of the Sarlacc pit? This question is answered in a *Book of Boba Fett* flashback: we see Boba scavenging a breathing tube from a dying stormtrooper in the creature's moist innards, before pulling himself slowly up and out of the sandy pit by hand. Seeing Morrison as Boba Fett crawl out of that trap in some ways symbolizes what the live-action streaming series creators seemed to be attempting—at least in part—that is, redeeming earlier stories as they return to them. Here one of live-action Star Wars' few significant characters of color

FIGURE 5.3   Boba Fett, with Fennec Shand, after he has recovered his armor in
The Book of Boba Fett (LUCASFILM)

(Temuera Morrison) evolves from performing a minor adversary (Jango Fett)
and a multitude of disposable troopers (his clones) to a warrior-hero who is
multidimensional, deeply talented, and—literally—fleshed out.

What happens to Boba next in this flashback, after he escapes the Sarlacc
and the Jawas steal his armor, takes the story into deeper territory. Even more
significantly, it begins to reverse harmful representations with another material
character group: the Tuskens. Before we analyze their reframing in live-action
Star Wars, it's important to understand the Tuskens' historical presentation
and function. These masked characters participate in the original and prequel
trilogies as non-/semi-human, nearly identical beings. They appeared to be
humanoid when introduced in the first Star Wars film; their heads were either
covered by, or composed of, layered cloth and metal bolts in place of eyes, with
fixed leather-and-metal mouths. Their voices sounded a bit like the barks of
sea lions. Referred to disparagingly as "Sand People," they serve the first Star
Wars story as a threatening menace: they knock Luke out, raid his speeder,
and dismember C-3PO. Luke and Obi-Wan avoid them by staying vigilant
and keeping inside, especially at night. Their ambiguity as a species is enabled
by material character distance—they do not have to conform to the shape of
a human face and so take an unusual structure. But their bodies are clearly
those of people, so while their strangeness poses engaging questions for the
audience, it also suggests—in the context of the story—they are brutes to be
feared. The Tuskens' reappearance in the prequel trilogy fleshes them out a bit

(we are shown a village with pets and families) but also presents them as even more violent and cruel than in the original trilogy. They serve as Anakin's temptation to anger and revenge after they kidnap and torture his mother in *Episode II: Attack of the Clones*. Both Anakin and his stepfather, the bereaved Cliegg Lars (Jack Thompson), call them animals. Later, Anakin confesses to murdering an entire Tusken village to avenge his mother's death. He frames it as a shameful betrayal of the Jedi code, in part because he killed women and children. If the Tuskens were unambiguously predatory non-humans, there might be no humanity upon which to hang Anakin's moral lapse, no concern about women and children. Their status as material characters who sit somewhere along the hierarchical continuum of creature and man serves the story's needs while posing ethical questions the story does not address (at least not in the prequels).

There are also racial and cultural stereotypes in the design and characterization of the Tuskens. Entertainment writer Jordan Maison wrote a 2022 article for the tech and science website, Gizmodo, entitled "How The Book of Boba Fett Evolved Star Wars' View of the Tuskens," partially drawing on his own perspective as a Native American. In the article, Maison analyzes how these characters evolved in the new streaming series, and how they operate within the context of their original presentation of the "Savage Indian" trope. He writes "Star Wars is essentially a 'Space Western' and the genre has long been a heavy influence on the franchise; taking on most of the familiar tropes in the process." He goes on to suggest that

> Nothing is more synonymous with older Western stories than Native Americans being the antagonists. They're the "savages" making trouble for the more "civilized" heroes looking to tame the wild countryside. In *A New Hope* (and the Prequels), nothing embodied this more than the Tusken Raiders. They fit the trope to the letter: from raids on the settlers, wantonly kidnapping people, and even animalistic behavior.
>
> *(Maison 2022)*

Maison also points out a particularly relevant comment made by George Lucas in reference to their concept design, and though he does not analyze Lucas's meaning with regard to the Tuskens' status as liminal humans/material characters, the following citation is particularly illuminating in relation to the duality of novel familiarity. It also points to how the power of distance undergirds the foundation of the Tuskens, and supports other reporting on Lucas's approach to imagining his galaxy:

> George Lucas himself said much of the Tusken look/design was based on the Bedouins, an Indigenous Arab tribe from the desert regions in North Africa. One of the driving ideas behind so many of the initial *Star*

Wars designs stemmed from taking something recognizable, but altering it into something new. In *A Gallery of Imagination: The Art of Ralph McQuarrie*, Lucas explains, "You look at that painting of the Tusken Raiders and the banthas, and you say, 'Oh yeah, Bedouins …' Then you look at it some more and say, 'Wait a minute, that's not right. Those aren't Bedouins, and what are those creatures back there?'"

(Maison 2022)

This view into the Tusken's design origins suggests that what I'm calling the duality of novel familiarity was part of Lucas's vision from the beginning. The familiarity emerges from a range of real-world images and ideas, obscured by their creative intermixing. According to Lucasfilm creative art manager Phil Szostak, this is the feeling Lucas desired for his audience as he planned many of the elements and designs of the first film: "you say 'I've seen that, it's World War II—but wait a minute—that isn't any kind of jet I've ever seen before.' I want the whole film to have that quality! … it should look very familiar but at the same time not be familiar at all" (Szostak 2020, 15). But we see how novel familiarity can also be problematic, particularly when creating a semi-human character with negative characteristics drawn from established stereotypes. The original "Sand People" projected various stereotypical qualities often harmfully attached to Arab peoples and Native Americans in Western entertainment. The other side of the duality, the novelty of amalgamation in their design and fictional cultural context, has the potential to obscure familiarity. Made-up creatures can offer plausible deniability for cultural appropriation given this creative mix-matching—i.e. the Tuskens ride fictional Banthas instead of camels or donkeys. But such cover—intentional or unconscious—doesn't ultimately work; criticisms of specific cultural stereotypes have compounded over decades of live-action Star Wars. There is a moral imperative for creators to consider the harm such appropriation causes, and the responsibility required of artists who draw inspiration from cultures that are not their own.

While the potencies of material characters have led to negative representations in some Star Wars characters, they can also be employed for more fleshed-out and complex characterizations—in effect, more positive representations aimed at repair. The unmasked Boba Fett acts as the audience's emissary into a reframing of the Tusken Raiders aka "Sand People" of Tatooine, an effort begun in *The Mandalorian*, which re-introduces the Tuskens as complex people with a rich history. Later, in *The Book of Boba Fett,* the Tuskens take an increasingly central role, and the audience is given a view into the domestic lives of one Tusken tribe. In a series of flashbacks during its first episode, we see how the Tuskens collect Boba as he lies on the desert floor (injured by the Sarlacc and desert exposure), drag him through the hot sands, then add him to their small collection of captives.

A turning point comes when Boba is digging for water pods in the desert sand, along with a child Tusken assigned to watch over him, when a six-armed sand creature emerges from beneath the desert floor and attacks them. Boba fights the creature and manages to kill it, saving the child, which earns him some degree of respect from his captives. Boba starts to learn and use their gestural language, and trust develops. He begins training with their lead warrior (Joanna Bennett) in the use of the gaffi stick in specialized combat. When Boba discovers that a train running through the desert has been attacking this Tusken village, he offers to team up in a planned offense. Boba steals a few speeders (Star Wars motorcycles) and, with the leader's permission, teaches the Tuskens to drive them. This provides counterpoint to the training the Tuskens are giving Boba in a kind of two-way exchange. The Tuskens and Boba together succeed in the battle to overcome the train and its drivers, whom Boba commands, to hereafter respect the Tusken's ancestral claim to their lands. As they sit by the fire after the victory, the Tusken leader shares more of their history with Boba, using a combination of verbal and gestural language. Via Boba's words and English subtitles, the audience learns that the Tuskens are native to Tatooine, and composed of a diverse range of smaller societies who have chosen different ways (sometimes through violence) to respond to the "off-world" settlers who have overtaken their lands, once rich with water. The story here is also creating/revealing the Tuskens as native victims of colonization—offering a new, fleshed-out history that didn't exist, but is suggested as having existed out of our view as audience members, and out of the view of the "off-world" humans.

After interviewing Temuera Morrison and his *Boba Fett* castmate, Ming-Na Wen, Yahoo Entertainment writer Ethan Alter wrote that the series is "reframing our collective understanding of Tatooine's nomadic sand people, the Tusken Raiders." He suggests that "both series instead position them as the planet's Indigenous population who are watching their native home and its resources be appropriated by would-be colonizers" (Alter 2022). What happens to Boba Fett in his final scenes with the Tuskens in *The Book of Boba Fett* holds multilayered significance in terms of representation as well. In being made an honorary member of the Tusken group, Boba is put on what appears to be a vision quest that leads to a personal awakening, coached in building his own gaffi stick and gifted with traditional Tusken garb. He appears reborn as a warrior and honorary member of the family and joins a ritualistic dance unifying the tribe around a fire. He is, at this point of the story, no longer a lone and self-serving mercenary hunter, covered in metal, but a member of a profoundly human society. The way he blends in and becomes—at least at a distance—indistinguishable from his companions in their circular dance echoes the conforming multitudes of the clones who wore Morrison's duplicated face in the prequels. By contrast, this is the face of an individual experiencing the very human feeling of belonging.

There is another way material character powers contribute to the dignification of the Tuskens that is worth highlighting: the use of language. The Tuskens' way of communicating in the streaming TV series seems part of a movement towards a fuller exploration of characters who appear by their materiality to be semi-human or at least ambiguously distanced from people. The Tuskens have fixed, mask-like mouths, which immediately suggests they speak differently than humans. This is part of the power of distance: it invites more open-minded attention to how intelligent beings can hold discourse. When the Tuskens appear in *The Mandalorian,* Din Djarin converses with them using both their spoken language and hand signs. This indicates a complexity to these material characters that's been hidden from audiences as well as the human characters, such as the Marshal (Timothy Olyphant) who gazes in wonder at his companion's social intercourse with these enemies of his village. The vocal and gestural conversations between the masked Din Djarin and the Tuskens also indicates a kind of two-pronged approach to interpersonal communication in this series developed further in *The Book of Boba Fett*. Boba Fett also learns the Tuskens' sign language as he begins to develop a friendly, ultimately familial relationship with the tribe. Both the masked Din Djarin and the unmasked Boba Fett act as translators to bring the audiences a fresh view of these iconic material characters, and the language used to make that translation is itself redemptive. Though the gestures look similar to sign language—what many Deaf communities in the real world use to communicate—it is actually a made-up language for use in Star Wars. But it wasn't appropriated; it was created by Oscar-winner actor Troy Kotsur, who is himself Deaf and a sign-language speaker. He both created the language and taught it to his castmates performing Tuskens in the streaming series (Abenchuchan 2020). The use of signing is presented in the series as a form of communication that can be used to broker agreements between different groups, sometimes with opposing goals. This is all woven into a story that redefines the Tuskens as intelligent beings with their own story to tell. As a Deaf actor performing a Tusken, Kostur brings broader representation to the cast as well as a new type of silent, gestural language to Star Wars.

These choices collectively reflect on and challenge live-action Star Wars' past presentation not just of the Tuskens themselves, but of the notion of the Native as Other and adversarial. Yet it's important to note that these changes are themselves full of nuance and complexity; they may not always have a positive outcome. Some fans have responded to the Boba—Tusken story as another example of the harmful "white savior" trope, given that Boba teaches them technology and helps save them from their oppressors. Entertainment writer Dais Johnston interviewed Star Wars fans from Indigenous cultures to get their perspective for their 2022 *Inverse* article "How Boba Fett's Tusken Raiders Subvert the White Savior Trope." In the article, Johnston analyzes some of the complexities in Tusken portrayals over decades, and the perspectives of fans who respond—which often depends on their own identity and lived experiences. Johnston reports that "Every Indigenous person interviewed for this story expressed frustration at the non-Indigenous fans who call *The Book of Boba Fett* a 'white savior' story." The interviewees' responses were varied, but the story shows a thematic interest in Temuera Morrison's embodied identity in his performance of Boba. Johnston writes "Boba Fett isn't white: Temuera Morrison, who portrays the character, is of Māori descent and, since he's not white, he can't be a *white* savior" (Johnston 2022). Fans Johnston interviewed reported feeling that

> by taking the trope and putting an Indigenous person at the center of it, Boba Fett turns the whole idea inside out. "It's playing with that white savior trope, but it's supposed to undermine it by having a Native man in that place," [a Navajo fan] tells Inverse. "And therefore it can be changed and is useful." Ali Nahdee agrees. "At this point, it's less savior and more solidarity."
>
> *(Johnston 2022)*

Ethan Alter writes about Morrison's participation in a similar way, describing how it shifts the meaning of the Boba-Tusken story from his point of view:

> That storyline resonates with Morrison, who traces his ancestry back to New Zealand's own Indigenous tribe, the Māori. "We know all about that word 'colonized,'" he says. "It's a great opportunity for me as a Māori from New Zealand to put us on the world stage again. I feel a sense of responsibility."
>
> *(Alter 2022)*

Peter Mutuc's 2022 *Screen Rant* article, "Temuera Morrison Completes His Claiming Of Boba Fett," contextualizes the actor's explanations of how he drew on his own training in the traditional Māori haka dance to perform the iconic Star Wars warrior. Mutuc connects Morrison's own cultural identity to the larger story of the reframed Tuskens this way:

> Elements of the Māori haka dance are also present in the scenes wherein Boba Fett and the Tusken Raiders perform a ritualistic dance around a bonfire. Apart from humanizing a race that has long functioned mainly as cannon fodder in previous Star Wars movies, the direct influence of Māori culture on the Tusken tribes and the backstory of Boba Fett practically embeds Morrison's very DNA into the iconic character. Moreover, the way the Tusken tribes are fighting for their ancestral domain also somewhat echoes the Māori protest movement for Indigenous sovereignty and self-determination, not just in New Zealand but across the

world. Through the careful use of Morrison's Māori heritage, *The Book of Boba Fett* succeeds at canonizing Morrison's influence on the iconic Star Wars character.

(Mutuc 2022)

Mutuc is here connecting the Tuskens to Boba to Morrison in a way that promotes both cultural respect and actor agency. Morrison incorporated traditional practices into the storytelling, which helped counter Star Wars' earlier practices of less engaged, less inclusive use of cultural images, artifacts, and practices—i.e., its habits of cultural appropriation.

The reframing and growth demonstrated in this new hope, this better direction for Star Wars is just that—a direction. There are still problems with the way material character powers are used to represent culture, race, and social structures. It's important to note that live-action Star Wars continues to use material characters as disposable Others that are less than human (the troopers Boba kills are human beings—and it's ironic that an iteration of his own face once inhabited such masks). Even in their elevated presence in the newer stories, many creatures demonstrate a Star Wars attitude that the non-human is somewhat disposable, and their forced service is ethical under certain circumstances. For example, the muscular green Gamorreans, with their human bodies and boar-like heads, have more screen time and attention in the subsequent series *The Book of Boba Fett* than they did in the original trilogy. But these fellows are written as servants asked to pledge life and loyalty to the human, Boba Fett, in order to save their own lives (and in that service, end up dead by the end of the first season). Changes point to opportunity, and they offer a map in framing the narrative around characters who might present or echo historically marginalized people (and I mean historically both in the real sense, and in the fictional world of Star Wars). Some of the Indigenous Star Wars fans interviewed by Dais Johnson offered their thoughts on the meaning that radiates out of the Tuskens' mass murder in *The Book of Boba Fett*. Some felt this a resonant reflection of traumatic historical events, such as the 1864 Sand Creek Massacre, and that the story did not take enough time to linger inside its meaning as Boba Fett enacted his funereal farewell. Some suggested that the series would do better to continue what they began in centering the Tuskens' story (Johnston 2022).

Though there is more work to be done going forward, the first two Star Wars live-action series, *The Mandalorian* and *The Book of Boba Fett*, demonstrate ways to elevate material characters not only by centering them in the stories, but expanding the complexity of how their powers are used. In doing this, and simultaneously better representing and engaging the global majority in creative leadership and casting, live-action Star Wars seems to be reflecting on its past. Such experimentation with ways material characters can counter harmful representations, rather than support them, offers hope.

Conclusion

This final chapter offers perspectives on how material characters can enact harm, and also collaborate in positive growth. The first two sections of this chapter examined how material character powers can call attention to negative real-world patterns and even reinforce or extend them. We began by analyzing how Star Wars droid service is framed and played out, and the opportunities for reflection they present. The second two sections considered racial representation in material characters, beginning with the absent presence of Asian characters, presented as one of Star Wars' problematic patterns (particularly with cultural appropriation). We unpacked the question of Jar Jar Binks' caricature as it relates to material character powers, as well as ways helmet-masks have engaged in representations of humanity and race in its troopers. The final section offered a new hope in considering how material characters began to take center frame in live-action Star Wars in the early 2020s via its first two streaming series, in part by reframing the past presentation of problematic characterizations, such as that of the Tuskens. What I ultimately endeavor to convey here is the potential for artists to leverage material characters to challenge stereotypes, hierarchies, and harmful tropes. Well-drawn material characters, whose powers are understood and thoughtfully engaged, can help confront the negative notion of Other-ness, in part because of their own ontological placement at the margins. But importantly, this analysis demonstrates how material characters' powers of representation can only work positively if their stories—what they are written to affect and experience—enable them to participate in meaningful engagement with the diversity of the human experience. Material characters may not be human, but they reflect essential elements of humanity, and have an important role to play in its future.

References

Abenchuchan, Alex. 2020. "Deaf Actor Troy Kotsur in Star Wars: The Mandalorian— The Daily Moth." *The Daily Moth*. https://www.dailymoth.com/blog/deaf-actor-troy-kostur-in-star-wars-the-mandalorian.

Adamczak, D. 2019. "The Phantom Menace Was Racist and Here is Why That Matters." *Contemporary Racism*. https://contemporaryracism.org/27658/the-phantom-menace-was-racist-and-here-is-why-that-matters/.

Alter, Ethan. 2022. "Temuera Morrison Says He Felt 'A Sense of Responsibility' to Bring His Māori Heritage to 'The Book of Boba Fett.'" YouTube. https://www.yahoo.com/now/temuera-morrison-ming-na-wen-the-book-of-boba-fett-star-wars-Māori-haka-220944530.html.

Child, Ben. 2021. "Racist trolls may think they own Star Wars, but the saga's diversity issues are not cut and dried." *The Guardian*. https://www.theguardian.com/film/2021/mar/05/star-wars-racism-trolls-kelly-marie-tran

Chow, Keith. 2018. "Go Asians: A History of AAPI Representation in 'Star Wars.'" *The Nerds of Color*. https://thenerdsofcolor.org/2018/05/10/go-asians-a-history-of-aapi-representation-in-star-wars/.

Godfrey, Gavin, and Luigi Novi. 2015. "The Actor Who Played Jar Jar Binks Is Not Sorry." *VICE.* https://www.vice.com/en/article/5gjddd/ahmed-best-jar-jar-binks-interview.

Harrison, Eric. 1999. "A Galaxy Far, Far Off Racial Mark?" *Los Angeles Times,* May 26, 1999. https://www.latimes.com/archives/la-xpm-1999-may-26-ca-40965-story.html

Howard, Ron, director. 2018. *Solo: A Star Wars Story.* Screenplay by Jonathan Kasdan and Lawrence Kasdan. Lucasfilm Ltd.

Intagliata, Christopher. 2011. "The Origin of the Word 'Robot.'" *Science Friday.* https://www.sciencefriday.com/segments/the-origin-of-the-word-robot/#segment-transcript.

Johnston, Dais. 2022. "Indigenous Star Wars Fans Speak Out on the Tusken Raiders and 'White Savior' Claims." *Inverse.* https://www.inverse.com/entertainment/book-of-boba-fett-tusken-raiders-Indigenous.

Kornhaber, Spencer. 2018. "'Solo' Droid L3-37 Is the First Woke Bot of 'Star Wars.'" *The Atlantic,* May 27, 2018. https://www.theatlantic.com/entertainment/archive/2018/05/the-soul-of-solo-is-a-droid/560969/.

Maison, Jordan. 2022. "Book of Boba Fett's Tuskens: Star Wars' History with Native Rep." Gizmodo. https://gizmodo.com/how-the-book-of-boba-fett-evolved-star-wars-view-of-the-1848361263.

McIntosh, Jonathan. 2020. "The Tragedy of Droids in Star Wars." YouTube. https://www.youtube.com/watch?v=WD2UrB7zepo.

McIntosh, Jonathan. 2017. "The Stormtrooper Paradox." YouTube. https://www.youtube.com/watch?v=7L1QSYq2pUQ.

Mutuc, Peter. 2022. "Temuera Morrison Completes His Claiming Of Boba Fett." *Screen Rant.* https://screenrant.com/temuera-morrison-completes-claiming-boba-fett/.

Nelson, Victoria. 2003. *The Secret Life of Puppets.* Cambridge, MA: Harvard University Press.

Richards, Paulette. 2019. "'It's Not Easy Bein' Green': Greenface and the Jazzy Frog Trope," *Living Objects: African American Puppetry Essays*; 13. https://opencommons.uconn.edu/ballinst_catalogues/13.

Roth, Lane. 1980. "Bergsonian Comedy and Human Machines in Star Wars." *Film Criticism,* 4 (2) (Winter): 1–8. JSTOR.

Salisbury, Mark. 2018. *Moviemaking Magic of Star Wars: Creatures & Aliens.* New York, NY: Harry N. Abrams.

Szostak, Phil. 2018. *Art of Solo: A Star Wars Story.* New York, NY: Harry N. Abrams.

Szostak, Phil. 2020. "Introduction by Phil Szostak." In *The Art of Star Wars: The Rise of Skywalker,* 15–16. New York, NY: Abrams.

Wetmore, Kevin J. 2005. *The Empire Triumphant: Race, Religion and Rebellion in the Star Wars Films.* Jefferson, NC: McFarland. E-book.

Wheat, Alynda. 2000. "George Lucas' Jedi Mind Trick." *Salon.com,* March 22, 2000. https://www.salon.com/2000/03/22/lucas_2/.

EPILOGUE

At the beginning of this book, I promised to demonstrate the special powers material characters hold to make meaning, using live-action Star Wars characters as case studies. We've analyzed what material character powers are and how they've engaged with live-action Star Wars as an epic in ways minute and broad, helpful and harmful. We've considered how Star Wars presents the creature, droid, and masked figure as beautiful, strange, disposable, funny, adorable, and terrifying things that range in importance from the background extra to the chief villain or even, more recently, the hero.

Today, the original Star Wars films were a Long Time Ago themselves: despite supposedly taking place outside of our current time and culture, the 20th-century Star Wars attitudes, language, and even hairstyles are comically outdated, while the material characters have endured—both figuratively and in new forms. 1977's Darth Vader remains central to the live-action Star Wars epic; he has re-emerged in *Rogue One* and the streaming series *Obi-Wan Kenobi* looking much the way we left him (for he does not morph like Batman). Human characters get much resurrected in Star Wars as well, but those material ones have the ability to tether us to the epic not only with their reliable agelessness, but their almost limitless capacity to generate meaning back and forth across time.

I return now to C-3PO, who began Star Wars and helped begin this book. As a character performing human-ness, C-3PO is on the outside looking in at us, and yet he is so very human in his befuddled reactions to the way we behave. The combined qualities of being brilliantly knowledgeable and socially awkward make him more sympathetic, as so many of us are like that (or love someone who is). C-3PO's relationships to humans like Luke Skywalker make for an interesting person-thing balance in fantastical storytelling, but they also

DOI: 10.4324/9781003137559-8

offer us a suggestion. Perhaps we may need to find balance in the real world as well, given how much people rely on creatures and machines. Perhaps our playing with new varieties of made-up creatures and things, with appreciation for their powers and contributions, can suggest where those relationships might productively go. Fictional creatures performed with dignity and intelligence might help us reconsider our human-centered views and treatment of other organic beings, as well as our machines and objects (as John Bell and many other puppetry scholars have proposed). I hope that these tools I've shared for analyzing and appreciating material characters will inspire more curiosity about the human-material connection and its evolution. I've offered the beginnings of inquiries others should find useful to take up in the fields of posthumanism, robot ethics, disposability studies, material culture, and perhaps disciplines yet to come.

Material characters are powerful, and they have a great deal to teach us. May their force be with you.

STAR WARS LIVE-ACTION GUIDE

Listed chronologically in release order

Original Trilogy:

    Star Wars: Episode IV— A New Hope (1977)
Written and directed by George Lucas

    Star Wars: Episode V—The Empire Strikes Back (1980)
Directed by Irvin Kershner
Written by Leigh Brackett and Lawrence Kasdan
Story by George Lucas

    Star Wars: Episode VI—Return of the Jedi (1983)
Directed by Richard Marquand
Written by Lawrence Kasdan and George Lucas

Prequel Trilogy:

    Star Wars: Episode I—The Phantom Menace (1999)
Written and directed by George Lucas

    Star Wars: Episode II—Attack of the Clones (2002)
Directed by George Lucas
Written by Jonathan Hales and George Lucas

    Star Wars: Episode III—Revenge of the Sith (2005)
Written and directed by George Lucas

Sequel Trilogy:

Star Wars: Episode VII—The Force Awakens (2015)
Directed by J.J. Abrams
Written by J.J. Abrams, Michael Arndt and Lawrence Kasdan
Based on characters created by George Lucas

Star Wars: Episode VIII—The Last Jedi (2017)
Written and directed by Rian Johnson
Based on characters created by George Lucas

Star Wars: Episode IX—The Rise of Skywalker (2019)
Directed by J.J. Abrams
Written by J.J. Abrams and Chris Terrio
Based on characters created by George Lucas

Star Wars Stories:

Rogue One: A Star Wars Story (2016)
Directed by Gareth Edwards
Written by Tony Gilroy and Chris Weitz
Based on characters created by George Lucas

Solo: A Star Wars Story (2018)
Directed by Ron Howard
Written by Jonathan Kasdan and Lawrence Kasdan
Based on characters created by George Lucas

Referenced Disney+ series:

The Mandalorian (2019–)
Created by Jon Favreau
Based on STAR WARS by George Lucas
Season 1–2
Episode directors: Deborah Chow, Jon Favreau, Dave Filoni, Rick Fumuyiwa, Bryce Dallas Howard, Peyton Reed, Robert Rodriguez, Taika Waititi, and Carl Weathers.
Episode writers: Jon Favreau, Dave Filoni, Rick Fumuyiwa, Christopher Yost

The Book of Boba Fett (2021–2022)
Created by Jon Favreau
Based on STAR WARS by George Lucas

Episode directors: Dave Filoni, Steph Green, Bryce Dallas Howard, Robert Rodriguez, and Kevin Tancharoen

Episode writers: Jon Favreau, Dave Filoni, Noah Kloor

Obi-Wan Kenobi (2022)

Directed by Deborah Chow

Episode writers: Hossein Amini, Stuart Beattie, Hannah Friedman, Joby Harold, Andrew Stanton

All credits sourced from IMDb, The Internet Movie Database: https://www.imdb.com

BIBLIOGRAPHY

Abenchuchan, Alex. 2020. "Deaf Actor Troy Kotsur in Star Wars: The Mandalorian—The Daily Moth." *The Daily Moth.* https://www.dailymoth.com/blog/deaf-actor-troy-kostur-in-star-wars-the-mandalorian.

Abrams, J.J., director. 2015. *Star Wars: Episode VII—The Force Awakens.* Screenplay by Lawrence Kasdan, J.J. Abrams, and Michael Arndt. Lucasfilm Ltd.

Abrams, J.J., director. 2019. *Star Wars: Episode IX—The Rise of Skywalker.* Screenplay by J.J. Abrams, and Chris Terrio. Lucasfilm Ltd.

Adamczak, D. 2019. "The Phantom Menace Was Racist and Here is Why That Matters." *Contemporary Racism.* https://contemporaryracism.org/27658/the-phantom-menace-was-racist-and-here-is-why-that-matters/.

Alexander, Julia. 2017. "Star Wars: The Last Jedi is Divisive, but Kylo Ren Shouldn't Be." *Polygon.* https://www.polygon.com/2017/12/18/16791400/star-wars-the-last-jedi-kylo-ren-adam-driver-spoilers.

Alter, Ethan. 2022. "Temuera Morrison Says He Felt 'A Sense of Responsibility' to Bring his Māori Heritage to 'The Book of Boba Fett.'" YouTube. https://www.yahoo.com/now/temuera-morrison-ming-na-wen-the-book-of-boba-fett-star-wars-maori-haka-220944530.html.

Amato, Felice. 2016. "A Split Broom for Legs: An Amateur Looks at the Puppet as Material Allegory." *Puppetry International,* Spring and Summer, 39. 26–8.

Arnold, Gary. 1977. "'Star Wars' (PG)." *The Washington Post,* May 25, 1977. https://www.washingtonpost.com/wp-srv/style/longterm/movies/review97/starwarsarnold.htm.

Asch, Leslee. 2020. *Out of the Shadows: The Henson Festivals and Their Impact on Contemporary Puppet Theater,* edited by Nancy Moore and Sharon K. Emanuelli. Greenwich, CT: InForm Press.

Baruh, Brad, director. 2020. *Disney Gallery: The Mandalorian.* Season 1, Episode 5, "Practical." Disney.

Bass, Eric. 2014. "Visual Dramaturgy: Some Thoughts for Puppet Theatre-Makers." In *The Routledge Companion to Puppetry and Material Performance,* edited by Dassia N. Posner, John Bell, Claudia Orenstein, 54–60. New York, NY: Routledge.

Becker, Edith, and Kevin Burns, directors. 2004. *Empire of Dreams: The Story of the 'Star Wars' Trilogy*. https://subslikescript.com/movie/Empire_of_Dreams_ The_Story_of_the_Star_Wars_Trilogy-416716.

Beckwith, Ryan T. 2017. *Star Wars: 40 Years of the Force*. New York, NY: Time Books.

Bell, John. 2013. *American Puppet Modernism: Essays on the Material World in Performance*. New York, NY: Palgrave Macmillan.

Bell, John. 2014. "Playing with the Eternal Uncanny: The Persistent Life of Lifeless Objects." In *The Routledge Companion to Puppetry and Material Performance*, edited by Claudia Orenstein, Dassia N. Posner, and John Bell. New York, NY: Routledge.

Bell, John. 2021. "Unbounded in Time: Puppets and Epics." *Puppetry International*, Fall and Winter, (50): 4–6.

Bennett, Jane. 2010. *Vibrant Matter: A Political Ecology of Things*. Durham, NC: Duke University Press.

Blumenthal, Eileen. 2005. *Puppetry: A World History*. New York, NY: Harry N. Abrams.

Brooker, Will. 2020. *Star Wars*. London, UK: Bloomsbury Academic.

Burns, Kevin, director. 2007. *Star Wars: The Legacy Revealed*. Prometheus Entertainment, the History Channel.

Carlin, Shannon. 2019. "Baby Yoda Was the Most Googled Baby of 2019 & It's a Mood." *Bustle*. https://www.bustle.com/p/baby-yoda-was-the-most-googled-baby-of-2019-its-a-mood-19443446.

Child, Ben. 2021. "Racist trolls may think they own Star Wars, but the saga's diversity issues are not cut and dried." *The Guardian*. https://www.theguardian.com/film/2021/mar/05/star-wars-racism-trolls-kelly-marie-

Chitwood, Adam. 2020. "The Mandalorian Season 2 Finale Explained: Why It Nailed the Ending." Collider. https://collider.com/the-mandalorian-season-2-finale-ending-explained/.

Chow, Deborah, director. 2022. *Obi-Wan Kenobi*. Lucasfilm Ltd.

Chow, Keith. 2018. "Go Asians: A History of AAPI Representation in 'Star Wars.'" *The Nerds of Color*. https://thenerdsofcolor.org/2018/05/10/go-asians-a-history-of-aapi-representation-in-star-wars/.

Clark, Mark. 2015. *Star Wars FAQ: Everything Left to Know About the Trilogy That Changed the Movies*. Milwaukee, WI: Hal Leonard.

Daniels, Anthony. 2019. *I Am C-3PO: The Inside Story: Foreword by J.J. Abrams*. London, UK: DK.

Dircks, Phyllis T. 2004. *American Puppetry*. Jefferson, NC: McFarland.

Ebert, Roger. 1997. *The Empire Strikes Back Movie Review (1997)*. Roger Ebert, April 1, 1997. https://www.rogerebert.com/reviews/the-empire-strikes-back-1997-1.

Edwards, Gareth, director. 2016. *Rogue One: A Star Wars Story*. Screenplay by Tony Gilroy and Chris Weitz. Lucasfilm Ltd.

Emigh, John. 1996. *Masked Performance: The Play of Self and Other in Ritual and Theatre*. Philadelphia, PA: University of Pennsylvania Press.

Evans, Nick. 2017. "Why Star Wars: The Last Jedi Made the Decision about Kylo Ren's Mask." *CinemaBlend*, December 26, 2017. https://www.cinemablend.com/news/1751099/why-star-wars-the-last-jedi-made-the-decision-about-kylo-rens-mask.

Failes, Ian. 2015. *Masters of FX: Behind the Scenes with Geniuses of Visual and Special Effects*. Hachette, UK: Ilex.

Favreau, Jon, creator 2019. *The Mandalorian*. Lucasfilm Ltd.

Favreau, Jon, creator. 2019. *The Book of Boba Fett*. Lucasfilm Ltd.

Finch, Christopher. 1993. *Jim Henson: The Works: The Art, the Magic, the Imagination*. New York, NY: Random House Publishing Group.

Francis, Penny. 2012. *Puppetry: A Reader in Theatre Practice*. New York, NY: Bloomsbury Academic.

Giardina, Carolyn. 2018. "How 'Last Jedi' Used Real-World Animals to Create CG Porgs." *The Hollywood Reporter*, January 3, 2018. https://www.hollywoodreporter.com/movies/movie-news/how-last-jedi-used-real-world-animals-create-cg-porgs-1071139/.

Godfrey, Gavin, and Luigi Novi. 2015. "The Actor Who Played Jar Jar Binks Is Not Sorry." *VICE*. https://www.vice.com/en/article/5gjddd/ahmed-best-jar-jar-binks-interview.

Gross, Kenneth. 2011. *Puppet: An Essay on Uncanny Life*. Chicago, IL: University of Chicago Press.

Gross, Kenneth. 2014. "Foreword." In *The Routledge Companion to Puppetry and Material Performance*, edited by Dassia N. Posner, John Bell, and Claudia Orenstein, xxiii. New York, NY: Routledge.

Grossman, Lev. 2015. "A New Hope: How J.J. Abrams Brought Back Star Wars Using Puppets, Greebles and Yak Hair." *TIME Magazine*, December 14, 2015, 56–75.

Grossman, Lev. 2019. "Star Wars Episode IX: The Rise of Skywalker." *Vanity Fair*, Summer, 2019, 80–105.

Harrison, Eric. 1999. "A Galaxy Far, Far Off Racial Mark?" *Los Angeles Times*, May 26, 1999.

Hibberd, James. 2019. "'The Mandalorian' Unmasked: 'We Did Things No "Star Wars" Fan Has Ever Seen.'" *Entertainment Weekly*, September 5, 2019. https://ew.com/tv/2019/09/05/inside-the-mandalorian-star-wars/.

Howard, Ron, director. 2018. *Solo: A Star Wars Story*. Screenplay by Jonathan Kasdan and Lawrence Kasdan. Lucasfilm Ltd.

IMDb: Ratings, Reviews, and Where to Watch the Best Movies & TV Shows. Accessed December 3, 2022. https://www.imdb.com/.

Intagliata, Christopher. 2011. "The Origin of The Word 'Robot.'" *Science Friday*. https://www.sciencefriday.com/segments/the-origin-of-the-word-robot/#segment-transcript.

Jameson, A.D. 2018. *I Find Your Lack of Faith Disturbing: Star Wars and the Triumph of Geek Culture*. New York, NY: Farrar, Straus and Giroux.

Johnson, Rian, director. 2017. *Star Wars: Episode VIII—The Last Jedi*. Screenplay by Rian Johnson. Lucasfilm Ltd.

Johnston, Dais. 2022. "Indigenous Star Wars Fans Speak Out on the Tusken Raiders and 'White Savior' Claims." *Inverse*. https://www.inverse.com/entertainment/book-of-boba-fett-tusken-raiders-indigenous.

Jones, Basil. 2014. "Puppetry, Authorship, and the Ur-Narrative." In *The Routledge Companion to Puppetry and Material Performance*, edited by Dassia N. Posner, John Bell, Claudia Orenstein, 61–68. New York, NY: Routledge.

Jones, Brian J. 2017. *George Lucas: A Life*. Boston, MA: Little, Brown.

Kamp, David. 2017. "Star Wars; 1977–2017, May the 40th Be With You!" *Vanity Fair*, Summer, 2017, 80–101.

Kaplin, Stephen. 1999. "A Puppet Tree: A Model for the Field of Puppet Theatre." *TDR*, 43 (3) (Autumn): 28–36.

Kershner, Irvin, director. 1980. *Star Wars: Episode V—The Empire Strikes Back*. Screenplay by Leigh Brackett and Lawrence Kasdan. Lucasfilm Ltd.

Kornhaber, Spencer. 2018. "'Solo' Droid L3-37 Is the First Woke Bot of 'Star Wars.'" *The Atlantic*, May 27, 2018. https://www.theatlantic.com/entertainment/archive/2018/05/the-soul-of-solo-is-a-droid/560969/.

Kornhaber, Spencer. 2019. "'The Mandalorian' Season Finale Scrambles Man and Machine." *The Atlantic*, December 30, 2019. https://www.theatlantic.com/entertainment/archive/2019/12/mandalorian-season-finale-scrambles-man-and-machine/604237/.

Kushins, Josh. 2016. *The Art of Rogue One: A Star Wars Story*. New York, NY: Harry N. Abrams.

Life. 2022. *George Lucas and the Making of Star Wars*. New York, NY: Dotdash Meredith Premium Publishing.

Life. 2019. *Mister Rogers: The Magical World of an American Icon*. New York, NY: LIFE Books, Meredith Corporation.

Life. 2016. *Science Fiction; 100 Years of Great Movies*. Tampa, FL: LIFE Books.

Longworth, Karina. 2012. *Masters of Cinema: George Lucas*. Paris: Cahiers du cinéma.

Lucas, George, director. 1977. *Star Wars: Episode IV—A New Hope*. Screenplay by George Lucas. Lucasfilm Ltd.

Lucas, George. 1999. *George Lucas: Interviews*, edited by Sally Kline. Jackson, MS: University Press of Mississippi.

Lucas, George, director. 1999. *Star Wars: Episode I—The Phantom Menace*. Screenplay by George Lucas. Lucasfilm Ltd.

Lucas, George, director. 2002. *Star Wars: Episode II—Attack of the Clones*. Screenplay by Jonathan Hales and George Lucas. Lucasfilm Ltd.

Lucas, George, director. 2005. *Star Wars: Episode III—Revenge of the Sith*. Screenplay by George Lucas. Lucasfilm Ltd.

Lucas, George, and Lawrence Kasdan. 1997. *The Art of Return of the Jedi, Star Wars: Including the Complete Script of the Film by Lawrence Kasdan and George Lucas*, edited by Lawrence Kasdan and George Lucas. New York, NY: Ballantine Books.

Lyne, Chris. 2019. "Complete Breakdown of the Entire Empire Magazine Article about 'Star Wars: The Rise of Skywalker.'" Star Wars News Net. https://www.starwarsnewsnet.com/2019/10/rise-skywalker-abrams-terrio-empire.html.

Madrigal, Alexis C. 2014. "The Remarkable Way Chewbacca Got a Voice." *The Atlantic*, August 7, 2014. https://www.theatlantic.com/technology/archive/2014/08/the-remarkable-way-chewbacca-got-a-voice/375697/.

Maison, Jordan. 2022. "Book of Boba Fett's Tuskens: Star Wars' History with Native Rep." Gizmodo. https://gizmodo.com/how-the-book-of-boba-fett-evolved-star-wars-view-of-the-1848361263.

Marikar, Sheila. 2010. "The Top 10 Worst TV and Film Characters." *ABC News*. https://abcnews.go.com/Entertainment/Movies/top-10-worst-tv-film-characters-time/story?id=10809609.

Marquand, Richard, director. 1983. *Star Wars: Episode VI—Return of the Jedi*. Screenplay by Lawrence Kasdan and George Lucas. Lucasfilm Ltd.

McIntosh, Jonathan. 2020. "The Tragedy of Droids in Star Wars." YouTube. https://www.youtube.com/watch?v=WD2UrB7zepo.

McIntosh, Jonathan. 2017. "The Stormtrooper Paradox." YouTube. https://www.youtube.com/watch?v=7L1QSYq2pUQ.

Millet, Lydia. 2002. "Becoming Darth Vader." In *A Galaxy Not So Far Away: Writers and Artists on Twenty-Five Years of Star Wars*, edited by Glenn Kenny. New York, NY: Henry Holt and Company.

Mutuc, Peter. 2022. "Temuera Morrison Completes His Claiming Of Boba Fett." *Screen Rant*. https://screenrant.com/temuera-morrison-completes-claiming-boba-fett/.

Nelson, Victoria. 2001. *The Secret Life of Puppets*. Cambridge, MA: Harvard University Press.

Nittle, Nadra K. 2021. "5 Common Indigenous Stereotypes in Film and Television." *ThoughtCo*. https://www.thoughtco.com/native-american-stereotypes-in-film-television-2834655.

Nutu, Ada. 2013. "Alterity and Puppets in Contemporary Performance." *Theatrical Colloquia (Colocvii teatrale)*, (15): 200–216. Central and Eastern European Online Library.

O'Connell, Mark. 2018. *Watching Skies: Star Wars, Spielberg and Us*. Gloucestershire, UK: History Press.

Orenstein, Claudia. 2014. "Introduction: A Puppet Moment." In *The Routledge Companion to Puppetry and Material Performance*, edited by Dassia N. Posner, John Bell, Claudia Orenstein, 2–4. New York, NY: Routledge.

Orenstein, Claudia. 2017. "Our Puppets, Our Selves: Puppetry's Changing Paradigms." *Mime Journal*, 26 (12) (February): 91–110.

Page, Ben, director. 2020. *Beyond Baby Yoda—The World of Puppets*. YouTube. https://www.youtube.com/watch?v=YDAO6KGaqcc.

Paska, Roman. 2012. "Notes on Puppet Primitives and the Future of an Illusion." In *Puppetry: A Reader in Theatre Practice*, 136–140. New York, NY: Bloomsbury Academic.

Piris, Paul. 2014. "The Co-Presence and Ontological Ambiguity of the Puppet." In *The Routledge Companion to Puppetry and Material Performance*, edited by Dassia N. Posner, John Bell, Claudia Orenstein, 30–42. New York, NY: Routledge.

Platt College. n.d. "Star Wars | Visual Effects through the Years." Platt College San Diego. Accessed November 5, 2022. https://platt.edu/blog/a-breakdown-of-the-visual-effects-used-in-the-star-wars-franchise/#0.

Posner, Dassia N. 2014. "Introduction; Material Performance(s)." In *The Routledge Companion to Puppetry and Material Performance*, edited by Dassia N. Posner, John Bell, and Claudia Orenstein. New York, NY: Routledge.

Posner, Dassia N. 2014. "Life-Death and Disobedient Obedience: Russian Modernist Redefinitions of the Puppet." In *The Routledge Companion to Puppetry and Material Performance*, edited by Dassia N. Posner, Claudia Orenstein, John Bell, 130–143. New York, NY: Routledge.

Posner, Dassia N. 2014. "Part III: Contemporary Investigations and Hybridizations." In *The Routledge Companion to Puppetry and Material Performance*, edited by Claudia Orenstein, John Bell, and Dassia N. Posner, 225–8. New York, NY: Routledge.

Richards, Paulette. 2019. "'It's Not Easy Bein' Green": Greenface and the Jazzy Frog Trope," *Living Objects: African American Puppetry Essays*; 13. https://opencommons.uconn.edu/ballinst_catalogues/13

Richau, Amy. 2018. "The Introduction of Kylo Ren and the Meaning of a Mask." *StarWars.com*. https://www.starwars.com/news/the-introduction-of-kylo-ren-and-the-meaning-of-a-mask.

Rinzler, J. W. 2010. *The Making of Star Wars: The Empire Strikes Back*. New York, NY: Random House Worlds.

Roark, Carolyn D. 2009. *Research at the Ransom Center: Death and the Puppet*, blog post. Harry Ransom Center, Ransom Edition (Spring 2009).

Robb, Brian J. 2012. *A Brief Guide to Star Wars: The Unauthorized Inside Story of George Lucas's Epic*. Philadelphia, PA: Robinson.

Rodley, Ed, ed. 2006. *Star Wars: Where Science Meets Imagination*. Washington, DC: National Geographic Society.

Romano, Steven. 2015. "5 Recycled Star Wars Props and Costumes." *StarWars.com* https://web.archive.org/web/20190909213609/https://www.starwars.com/news/5-recycled-star-wars-props-and-costumes.

Roth, Lane. 1980. "Bergsonian Comedy and Human Machines in Star Wars." *Film Criticism* 4 (2) (Winter): 1–8.

Salisbury, Mark. 2018. *Moviemaking Magic of Star Wars: Creatures & Aliens*. New York, NY: Harry N. Abrams.

Schultz, Roger, Roberto Darío Pomo, and Michael L. Greenwald. 2001. *The Longman Anthology of Drama and Theater: A Global Perspective*, edited by Michael L. Greenwald. London, UK: Longman.

Schwartz, Gregory. 2021. "Ben Burtt, R2D2, and the Humanization of Synthesis in Sound Design." *Hii Magazine*. https://hii-mag.com/article/benburttr2d2.

Searls, Colette. 2014. "Unholy Alliances and Harmonious Hybrids: New Fusions in Puppetry and Animation." In *The Routledge Companion to Puppetry and Material Performance*, edited by Dassia N. Posner, John Bell, Claudia Orenstein, 294–307. New York, NY: Routledge.

Shershow, Scott C. 1995. *Puppets and "Popular" Culture*. Ithica, NY: Cornell University Press.

Smythe, Robert. 2012. "Peculiar Possibilities: Narrative Theory and Puppetry's Ability to Edit Reality." *Puppetry International*, Spring and Summer, (31): 4–7.

Sunstein, Cass R. 2016. *The World According to Star Wars*. New York, NY: William Morrow Publishers.

Szostak, Phil. 2015. *The Art of Star Wars: The Force Awakens*. New York, NY: Harry N. Abrams.

Szostak, Phil. 2017. *The Art of Star Wars: The Last Jedi*. New York, NY: Harry N. Abrams.

Szostak, Phil. 2018. *Art of Solo: A Star Wars Story*. New York, NY: Harry N. Abrams.

Szostak, Phil. 2020. *The Art of Star Wars: The Mandalorian*. New York, NY: Harry N. Abrams.

Szostak, Phil. 2020. *The Art of Star Wars: The Rise of Skywalker*. New York, NY: Harry N. Abrams.

Szostak, Phil. 2020. "Introduction by Phil Szostak." In *The Art of Star Wars: The Rise of Skywalker*, 15–16. New York, NY: Harry N. Abrams.

Szostak, Phil. 2021. *The Art of Star Wars: The Mandalorian (Season Two)*. New York, NY: Harry N. Abrams.

Taylor, Chris. 2015. *How Star Wars Conquered the Universe: The Past, Present, and Future of a Multibillion Dollar Franchise*. New York, NY: Basic Books.

Taylor, Jane, ed. 2009. *Handspring Puppet Company*. New York, NY: David Krut Pub.

Thompson, Ayanna. 2021. *Blackface*. New York, NY: Bloomsbury Publishing.

Thompson, Clive. 2014. "Why Do We Love R2-D2 and Not C-3PO?" *Smithsonian Magazine*, May 14, 2014. https://www.smithsonianmag.com/arts-culture/why-do-we-love-r2-d2-and-not-c-3po-180951176/.

Tillis, Steve. 1996. "The Actor Occluded: Puppet Theatre and Acting Theory." *Theatre Topics,* 6 (2): 109–119.

Turnock, Julie A. 2015. *Plastic Reality: Special Effects, Technology, and the Emergence of 1970s Blockbuster Aesthetics.* New York, NY: Columbia University Press.

Wetmore, Kevin J. 2005. *The Empire Triumphant: Race, Religion and Rebellion in the Star Wars Films.* Jefferson, NC: McFarland. E-book.

Wheat, Alynda. 2000. "George Lucas' Jedi Mind Trick." *Salon.com,* March 22, 2000. https://www.salon.com/2000/03/22/lucas_2/.

Whitbrook, James. 2019. "Star Wars Empire Strikes Back & Dark Crystal History Connection." Gizmodo. https://gizmodo.com/how-the-empire-strikes-back-helped-shape-the-look-of-th-1837516288.

White, Timothy. 1980. "'Star Wars': Slaves to the 'Empire.'" *Rolling Stone,* July 24, 1980. https://www.rollingstone.com/culture/culture-news/star-wars-slaves-to-the-empire-61931/.

Wikipedia, The Free Encyclopedia, s.v. "Jar Jar Binks." n.d. Accessed November 5, 2022. https://en.wikipedia.org/wiki/Jar_Jar_Binks#cite_note-1.

Williams, Margaret. 2007. "Including the Audience: The Idea of 'the Puppet' and the Real Spectator." *Australasian Drama Studies,* 51 (October), 119–132. International Index to Performing Arts.

Windham, Ryder, and Adam Bray. 2017. *Star Wars Stormtroopers: Beyond the Armor,* edited by Adam Bray. New York, NY: HarperCollins.

WIRED. 2022. "Every Stormtrooper in Star Wars Explained by Lucasfilm." YouTube. https://www.youtube.com/watch?v=m4LFX-RWfn4&list=PLh4sGfPOCWCu-vhQkhZ7O8YPFl3dw_OGJ4&index=29.

INDEX

Printed in the United States
by Baker & Taylor Publisher Services